KU-447-913

Pocket
SYDNEY
TOP SIGHTS · LOCAL LIFE · MADE EASY

Peter Dragicevich

In This Book

QuickStart Guide

Your keys to understanding the city – we help you decide what to do and how to do it

Need to Know
Tips for a smooth trip

Neighbourhoods
What's where

Explore Sydney

The best things to see and do, neighbourhood by neighbourhood

Top Sights
Make the most of your visit

Local Life
The insider's city

The Best of Sydney

The city's highlights in handy lists to help you plan

Best Walks
See the city on foot

Sydney's Best...
The best experiences

Survival Guide

Tips and tricks for a seamless, hassle-free city experience

Getting Around
Travel like a local

Essential Information
Including where to stay

Our selection of the city's best places to eat, drink and experience:

◉ **Sights**

⊗ **Eating**

◑ **Drinking**

✪ **Entertainment**

🄰 **Shopping**

These symbols give you the vital information for each listing:

🎵 Telephone Numbers	👪 Family-Friendly
🕓 Opening Hours	🐾 Pet-Friendly
🅿 Parking	🚌 Bus
⊖ Nonsmoking	🚢 Ferry
@ Internet Access	🚋 Tram
📶 Wi-Fi Access	🚆 Train
🥗 Vegetarian Selection	

Find each listing quickly on maps for each neighbourhood:

Bar Hemingway

16 ◑ Map p233, B2

Legend has it that Hemi
self, wielding a machine
erate this timber-pan
ered bar during
showpiece is a
en by Papa ar
town. Dress
s.com; Hôtel Rit
⊙6.30pm-2a

Lonely Planet Pocket Guides are designed to get you straight to the heart of the city.

Inside you'll find all the must-see sights, plus tips to make your visit to each one really memorable. We've split the city into easy-to-navigate neighbourhoods and provided clear maps so you'll find your way around with ease. Our expert authors have searched out the best of the city: walks, food, nightlife and shopping, to name a few. Because you want to explore, our 'Local Life' pages will take you to some of the most exciting areas to experience the real Sydney.

And of course you'll find all the practical tips you need for a smooth trip: itineraries for short visits, how to get around, and how much to tip the guy who serves you a drink at the end of a long day's exploration.

It's your guarantee of a really great experience.

Our Promise

You can trust our travel information because Lonely Planet authors visit the places we write about, each and every edition. We never accept freebies for positive coverage, so you can rely on us to tell it like it is.

QuickStart Guide 7

Explore Sydney 21

Worth a Trip:

QuickStart Guide

Welcome to Sydney

Canberra may be the capital, but Sydney is Australia's first city. The nation's birthplace is exuberant, sassy and stacks of fun. Brash and shallow? Whatever... Sydney's sunny self-confidence is reinforced by its famously picturesque harbour and beautiful beaches. And if it's ever feeling blasé about its natural assets, a dizzying whirl of shopping, dining and partying carries on regardless.

Annual Sydney to Hobart yacht race with Sydney Harbour Bridge (p28) in the background.
POMINOZ / SHUTTERSTOCK ©

Sydney
Top Sights

Sydney Opera House (p24)

Striking, unique, curvalicious – is there a sexier building on the planet? What goes on inside (opera, theatre, dance, concerts) is almost as interesting as the famous exterior.

Bondi Beach
(p134)

A quintessential Sydney experience, Bondi Beach offers munificent opportunities for lazing on the sand, languishing in bars and cafes, carving up the surf, splashing about in the shallows and swimming in sheltered pools.

Royal Botanic Garden (p26)

Although the bustle of the city couldn't be closer, this spacious garden is superbly tranquil – the only conspicuous traffic is the purposeful procession of ferries on the harbour.

Art Gallery of NSW
(p48)

The stately neoclassical facade of the Art Gallery of NSW doesn't divulge the exuberance of the collection within. Step inside and enter a world of creativity.

Sydney Harbour Bridge (p28)

Like the Opera House, Sydney's second most loved construction inhabits the intersection of practicality and great beauty. The harbour views it provides are magnificent.

Taronga Zoo (p44)

Even if every single one of Taronga Zoo's 4000 or so animals was hiding or on vacation, the ferry ride and the harbour views would still make for a fantastic day out.

Sydney Sea Life Aquarium (p70)

Well laid out and absolutely fascinating, this complex has an impressive array of gigantic sharks and rays. Don't miss a rare opportunity to get up close and personal with a dugong.

Australian Museum (p100)

Historical collections of minerals and bones compete with 'dangerous Australians' and dinosaurs in this grande dame of Sydney museums. The Aboriginal section is particularly interesting.

Sydney
Local Life

Insider tips to help you find the real cit

After checking out the tourist sights, take some time to see what the locals are up to – on the river, on the fringes of the harbour, and in the city's financial, political, educational and fashion districts.

A Journey up the Parramatta River (p42)

▶ River life
▶ Industrial sites

Circular Quay may seem like the heart of the city, but Sydney's geographical centre is actually 20km upstream in Parramatta. A ferry ride west displays a different side of the city, revealing historic working-class neighbourhoods and the remnants of riverside industry.

City Escapes (p50)

▶ Urban parks
▶ Imposing buildings

Macquarie St was the civic showcase of the early convict colony and it is no less so today.

Nearby Martin Place and Pitt St are (respectively) the city's main financial and retail strips. When the pace gets too hectic, the city's spacious parks provide solace.

Studying the University of Sydney (p82)

▶ Museums
▶ Student hang-outs

The large campus of Sydney Uni dominates the suburbs on the city's western flank. While its Hogwartsian stone walls may suggest primness and properness, that's quite far from the reality of Sydney student life.

A Saturday in Paddington (p118)

▶ Markets
▶ Cafes & bars

Paddington revels in its reputation as the city's fashion and art quarter, and although its boutiques may be struggling to compete with nearby megamalls, its leafy streets still offer plenty o neighbourhood charm.

Wandering Around Woolloomooloo (p122)

▶ Historic wharf
▶ Backstreet pubs

Woolloomooloo's rough-edged reputation has taker a beating in recent years. Once known for its sozzled seadogs, tough-as-nails

Woolloomooloo Finger Wharf (p123)

Paddington (p118)

ROBIN SMITH / GETTY IMAGES ©

dockworkers and randy marines, the Finger Wharf is now full of movie-star apartments, luxurious hotel rooms and top-dollar restaurants. Thankfully, the beer and pies remain.

A Day in Watsons Bay (p146)

▶ Beaches
▶ Views

This once remote fishing village has some of Sydney's best harbour beaches and most dramatic clifftop views. Ogle the city's priciest harbourside real estate on the ferry ride, then stake your claim to one of the neighbourhood's hidden beaches.

Other great places and ways to experience the city like a local:

Yum cha in Chinatown (p58)

Darlinghurst's gay scene (p112)

Strolling along the Corso in Manly (p154)

Barracking for the Sea Eagles in a Manly pub (p153)

Chippendale (p86)

Searching for black gold in Surry Hills (p110)

Sydney
Day Planner

Day One

Start at Circular Quay and head directly to the **Sydney Opera House** (p24). Circle around it and follow the shoreline into the **Royal Botanic Garden** (p26). Have a good look about and then continue around **Mrs Macquaries Point** (p27) and down to Woolloomooloo. Grab a pie at **Harry's Cafe de Wheels** (p123), a Sydney institution.

Head back up to the **Art Gallery of NSW** (p48). Take some time to explore the gallery then cross the **Domain** (p50) and cut through **Sydney Hospital** (p51) to Macquarie St. **Parliament House** (p51) is immediately to the right, while to the left is **Hyde Park Barracks Museum** (p54). Cross into **Hyde Park** (p51) and head straight through its centre, crossing Park St and continuing on to the **Anzac Memorial** (p55).

For dinner, catch a train to Central and wander up to the **Devonshire** (p107) in Surry Hills. Afterwards, if you haven't booked tickets for a play at **Belvoir** (p114), take a stroll along Crown St. There are plenty of good bars and pubs to stop at along the way.

Day Two

Catch the bus to **Bondi Beach** (p134) and spend some time swimming, strolling about and soaking it all in. Once you're done, take the clifftop path to **Tamarama Beach** (p138) and on to **Bronte Beach** (p138), where you can grab lunch at **Three Blue Ducks** (p162).

Continue on the coastal path through **Waverley Cemetery** (p138) and down to **Clovelly Beach** (p139). This is a great spot to stop for a swim or a snorkel. Continuing on you'll pass Gordons Bay and Dolphin Point before you arrive at **Coogee Beach** (p139). Stop for a drink at **Coogee Pavilion** (p143) then jump on board a bus back to Bondi Junction, where you can switch to the train network.

Everyone needs at least one trashy night up the Cross. Start with cocktails at **Jimmy Lik's** (p131) before dinner at **Ms G's** (p126). Top it up afterwards with a tipple at **Bootleg** (p131). Then **Sugarmill** (p128), **Kings Cross Hotel** (p128), **World Bar** (p129)…

Short on time?

We've arranged Sydney's must-sees into these day-by-day itineraries to make sure you see the very best of the city in the time you have available.

Day Three

☀️ Take the scenic ferry ride from Circular Quay to Watsons Bay. Walk up to the **Gap** (p147) to watch the waves pounding against the cliffs, then continue on to **Camp Cove** (p147) for a dip. Take the **South Head Heritage Trail** (p147) for sublime views of the city and the whole of the upper harbour. For lunch, pull up a pew with a view at the **Watsons Bay Beach Club** (p147).

☀️ Head back to Circular Quay and spend the afternoon exploring the Rocks. Start at the **Museum of Contemporary Art** (p32) and then head up to the **Rocks Discovery Museum** (p32). Continue through the Argyle Cut to Millers Point and wander up **Observatory Hill** (p32). Double back under the **Sydney Harbour Bridge** (p28).

🌙 If last night was your trashy night, make this your glamorous one. Book ahead for one of the upmarket Circular Quay restaurants and a show at the **Sydney Opera House** (p24). Finish up at **Opera Bar** (p37) or one of the old pubs in the Rocks, such as the **Lord Nelson** (p37) or **Hero of Waterloo** (p38).

Day Four

☀️ Have a stroll around the Darling Harbour waterfront and settle on whichever of the big attractions takes your fancy – perhaps the **Australian National Maritime Museum** (p73) or **Sydney Sea Life Aquarium** (p70). Each of these will easily fill up an entire morning. For a quick bite, pop up to **Central Baking Depot** (p59).

☀️ Make your way to Circular Quay and catch a ferry to **Taronga Zoo** (p45). Spend the afternoon enjoying the animals and the harbour views before heading back to your accommodation to freshen up for the night ahead.

🌙 Head to the Inner West for your last night in Sydney. After dinner at **Ester** (p88) in Chippendale, take a short cab ride up to King St in Newtown and cruise the late-night bookstores and bars.

Need to Know

For more information,
see Survival Guide (p181)

Currency
Australian dollar ($)

Language
English

Visas
The only visitors who do not require a visa in advance of arriving in Australia are New Zealanders.

Money
There are ATMs everywhere and major credit cards are widely accepted.

Mobile Phones
Most international phones will work on the Australian network and accept local SIM cards. Quad-band North American and Japanese handsets will work but need to be unlocked to accept a SIM.

Time
Eastern Standard Time (GMT/UTC plus 10 hours)

Plugs & Adaptors
Standard voltage is 220 to 240 volts AC (50Hz). Plugs are flat three-pin types, with the top two pins angled.

Tipping
If the service is good, it is customary to tip at restaurants (up to 10%) and in taxis (round up to the nearest dollar).

① Before You Go

Your Daily Budget

Budget less than $190
▸ Dorm beds $22–$52
▸ Hanging out at the beach or free sights
▸ Free hostel breakfasts, with burgers or cheap noodles for lunch and dinner: all up $15

Midrange $190–$320
▸ Private room with bathroom $100–$200
▸ Cafe breakfast and lunch: $15 each
▸ Two-course dinner with glass of wine $45

Top End more than $320
▸ Four-star hotel from $200
▸ Three-course dinner with wine in top restaurant $120–$200
▸ Opera ticket $150
▸ Taxis $50

Useful Websites
▸ **Destination NSW** (www.sydney.com) Official visitors' guide.

▸ **City of Sydney** (www.cityofsydney.nsw. gov.au) Visitor information.

▸ **Sydney Morning Herald** (www.smh.com. au) Daily newspaper.

▸ **Lonely Planet** (www.lonelyplanet.com/ sydney) Destination information.

Advance Planning

Three months prior Book accommodation; make sure your passport, visa and travel insurance are in order.

One month prior Book top restaurants; check to see if your visit coincides with any major events or shows and book tickets.

A week prior Check the Sydney news sites and what's-on lists.

② Arriving in Sydney

The vast majority of visitors to Sydney arrive at Sydney Airport (☎02-9667 9111; www. sydneyairport.com.au; Airport Dr, Mascot), also known as Kingsford Smith Airport, 10km south of the city centre. Long-distance trains chug into Sydney's Central station.

✈ From Sydney Airport

Destination	Best Transport
Circular Quay & the Rocks	Sydney Airporter Shuttle
City Centre	Sydney Airporter Shuttle
Newtown	Taxi
Bondi	Taxi
Manly	Manly Express Shuttle

✈ At the Airport

Sydney Airport The airport has separate international (T1) and domestic (T2 and T3) terminals, 4km apart on either side of the runway. Each has eateries, left-luggage services, ATMs, currency-exchange bureaux and rental-car counters. The international terminal offers plenty of opportunity for duty-free shopping.

③ Getting Around

Visitors should find Sydney's public transport easy to use and reasonably efficient. You're best to obtain an Opal smartcard (free from newsagents; p185) and load money on to it for use on trains, buses, ferries and trams.

🚆 Train

Generally the best way to get around, with reliable and reasonably frequent central services.

🚌 Bus

Buses will get you to all the places that trains don't go, such as the Eastern Beaches and Vaucluse.

🚊 Light Rail

Connects Central station, Pyrmont and Glebe, but nowhere else you're likely to go.

⛴ Ferry

An excellent way to see the harbour and the best option for getting from the city to Manly, Watsons Bay, Taronga Zoo, Cockatoo Island and Balmain.

🚗 Car

Handy for getting to the beaches, but a liability around the central city due to hefty parking charges.

🚗 Taxi

Reasonably priced for short trips around central neighbourhoods.

🚤 Water Taxi

Expensive but quick and flexible way of getting around the harbour.

Sydney
Neighbourhoods

**Circular Quay &
The Rocks (p22)**
The historic heart of
Sydney, containing its
most famous sights.
◉ Top Sights
Sydney Opera House

Royal Botanic Garden

Sydney Harbour Bridge

**City Centre &
Haymarket (p46)**
Sydney's central
business district offers
plenty of choices for
shopping, eating and
sightseeing, with colonial
buildings scattered
among the skyscrapers.
◉ Top Sights
Art Gallery of NSW

**Darling Harbour &
Pyrmont (p68)**
Unashamedly tourist
focused, Darling
Harbour tempts visitors
to its shoreline bars and
restaurants with
fireworks displays and a
sprinkling of glitz.
◉ Top Sights
Sydney Sea Life Aquarium

Inner West (p80)
Quietly bohemian Glebe
and more loudly
bohemian Newtown are
the most well known of
the Inner West's tightly
packed suburbs,
grouped around the
University of Sydney.

*Sydney
Harbour
Bridge*

*Sydney
Opera
House* ◉

◉ *Royal
Botanic
Garden*

*Art Gallery
of NSW* ◉

*Sydney
Sea Life
Aquarium*

◉
*Australian
Museum*

Kings Cross & Potts Point (p120)

Strip joints, tacky tourist shops and backpacker hostels bang heads with classy restaurants, boozy bars and gorgeous guesthouses as 'the Cross' pumps 24/7.

Manly (p148)

The only place in Sydney where you can catch a ferry to swim in the ocean, Manly caps off the harbour with scrappy charm.

Worth a Trip

⊙ Top Sights

Taronga Zoo

⊙ *Taronga Zoo*

Surry Hills & Darlinghurst (p98)

Home to a mishmash of inner-city hipsters, yuppies, a large gay and lesbian community, and an array of excellent bars and eateries.

⊙ Top Sights

Australian Museum

Bondi to Coogee (p132)

Improbably good-looking arcs of sand framed by jagged cliffs, the Eastern Beaches are a big part of the Sydney experience.

⊙ Top Sights

Bondi Beach

⊙ *Bondi Beach*

Explore
Sydney

Worth a Trip

Bondi Beach (p134) promenade
MANFRED GOTTSCHALK / GETTY IMAGES ©

Explore

Circular Quay & The Rocks

The birthplace of both the city and the nation, this compact area seamlessly combines the historic with the exuberantly modern. Circular Quay's promenade serves as a backdrop for buskers of mixed merit and locals disgorging from harbour ferries. Join the tourist pilgrimage to the Opera House and Harbour Bridge, then grab a pint at a convict-era pub in the Rocks.

The Sights in a Day

Start at Circular Quay and head directly to the **Sydney Opera House** (p24). Follow the shoreline into the **Royal Botanic Garden** (p26), then continue to **Mrs Macquaries Point**. When you've seen enough, backtrack to Circular Quay and call in to the **Customs House** (p32). Continue around Circular Quay and pop up to **Sailors Thai Canteen** (p36) for lunch.

Spend the afternoon exploring the Rocks. Start at the **Museum of Contemporary Art** (p32) and then head up into the network of narrow lanes to the **Rocks Discovery Museum** (p32) and **Susannah Place** (p32). Continue through the Argyle Cut to Millers Point and wander up the hill to **Sydney Observatory** (p32). Pop into one of Sydney's oldest pubs, perhaps the **Lord Nelson Brewery Hotel** (p37), and then cut down to **Walsh Bay** (p34) and double back under the **Harbour Bridge** (p28).

Book well in advance for Sydney's top restaurant, **Quay** (p35), followed by a show at the Opera House or Walsh Bay. Otherwise, head to **Opera Bar** (p37) to be mesmerised by the lights sparkling on the water.

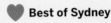 **Top Sights**

Sydney Opera House (p24)

Royal Botanic Garden (p26)

Sydney Harbour Bridge (p28)

♥ Best of Sydney

Eating
Quay (p35)

Bars & Pubs
Lord Nelson Brewery Hotel (p37)

Opera Bar (p37)

Hero of Waterloo (p38)

Blu Bar on 36 (p39)

Historic Buildings
Government House (p27)

Customs House (p32)

Susannah Place (p32)

Getting There

🚆 **Train** Circular Quay is one of the City Circle stations.

⛴ **Ferry** Circular Quay is Sydney's ferry hub and has services to Watsons Bay, Manly, Taronga Zoo, Darling Harbour, Cockatoo Island and Balmain, among others.

🚌 **Bus** Several bus routes terminate at Circular Quay, including services to/from Glebe, Newtown, Surry Hills, Darlinghurst, Kings Cross, Paddington, Bondi, Coogee and Watsons Bay.

Top Sights
Sydney Opera House

Gazing upon the Sydney Opera House with virgin eyes is a sure way to send a tingle down your spine. Danish architect Jørn Utzon's competition-winning 1956 design is Australia's most recognisable visual image. Gloriously white, curvaceous and pointy, it perches dramatically at the tip of Bennelong Point, waiting for its close-up. No matter from which angle you point a lens at it, this beauty shamelessly mugs for the camera; it really doesn't have a bad side.

◉ Map p30, E2

☎ 02-9250 7250

www.sydneyoperahouse.com

Bennelong Point

tours adult/child $37/20

⊙ tours 9am-5pm

🚆 Circular Quay

Concert Hall

Don't Miss

Exterior

The House's dramatic shape is thought to have been inspired by billowing sails. It's not until you get close that you realise that the seemingly solid expanse of white is actually composed of tiles; 1,056,000 self-cleaning, cream-coloured Swedish tiles, to be exact.

Performances

Dance, concerts, opera and theatre are staged in the Concert Hall, Joan Sutherland Theatre, Drama Theatre and Playhouse, while more intimate and left-of-centre shows inhabit the Studio. The acoustics in the Concert Hall are superb. Companies that regularly perform here include Opera Australia, Sydney Theatre Company, Bangarra Dance Theatre and the Australian Ballet.

Tours

The interiors don't live up to the promise of the dazzling exterior, but if you're curious to see inside, one-hour guided tours depart half-hourly. For a more in-depth look, the two-hour early morning backstage tour ($165, departs 7am) includes the Green Room and dressing rooms.

Utzon Room

The interior of this room is the only one to have been designed by Utzon, before he quit the project in disgust in 1966. Construction of the building started in 1959 but after delays, politicking and cost blowouts, the Opera House finally opened in 1973. Utzon died in 2008 having never seen his finished masterpiece in the flesh.

☑ Top Tips

▶ Most performances (2400 of them annually) sell out quickly, but partial-view tickets are often available on short notice.

▶ You'll save 10% on tours if you book online.

▶ Not all tours can visit all theatres because of rehearsals, but you're more likely to see everything if you go early.

▶ Kids at the House is a pint-sized entertainment roster of music, drama and dance.

✗ Take a Break

Call into Opera Bar (p37) on the lower concourse on the Circular Quay side of the Opera House for an alfresco beverage and dazzling harbour views.

As well as being in charge of the food at Opera Bar, celebrity chef Matt Moran's signature fine-dining restaurant Aria (p36) is situated right at the end of East Circular Quay, in the closest possible proximity to the Opera House.

Top Sights
Royal Botanic Garden

This expansive park is the inner city's favourite picnic destination, jogging route and snuggling spot. Bordering Farm Cove, immediately east of the Sydney Opera House, the garden was established in 1816 and features plant life from Australia and around the world. It includes the site of the colony's first paltry vegetable patch, but its history goes back much further than that; long before the convicts arrived this was an initiation ground for the Gadigal people.

Map p30, F4

02-9231 8111

www.rbgsyd.nsw.gov.au

Mrs Macquaries Rd

admission free

7am-8pm Oct-Feb, to 5.30pm Mar-Sep

Circular Quay

Don't Miss

Plants

Highlights include the **rose garden**, the **rainforest walk** and the **succulent garden**. There are also a begonia garden, herb garden, palm grove, pioneer garden, rare and threatened plants garden, bushland walk, Australian native rockery, fernery and an ever-popular camellia garden. The garden's many magnificent mature trees are well labelled with genus and place of origin.

Government House

Encased in English-style grounds within the garden, **Government House** (☎02-9931 5222; www.sydneylivingmuseums.com.au; Macquarie St; admission free; ◷grounds 10am-4pm, tours 10.30am-3pm Fri-Sun; ℞Circular Quay) is the official residence of the Governor of NSW. This Gothic sandstone palace is also used for hosting visiting heads of state and royalty. The interior can be accessed on a free guided tour.

Mrs Macquaries Point

Adjoining the gardens, Mrs Macquaries Point forms the northeastern tip of Farm Cove and provides beautiful views over the bay to the Opera House and city skyline. It was named in 1810 after Elizabeth, Governor Macquarie's wife, who ordered a seat chiselled into the rock from which she could view the harbour.

Tours

Free 1½-hour guided walks depart at 10.30am daily from the information booth outside the Gardens Shop. From March to November there's also an additional hour-long tour at 1pm on weekdays. Book ahead for an **Aboriginal Heritage Tour** (☎02-9231 8134; adult/child $37/17; ◷10am Fri), which covers local history, traditional plant uses and bush-food tastings.

☑ **Top Tips**

▶ If you're all walked out, take a ride on the **Choochoo Express** (Map p30, E2; www.choochoo.com.au; adult/child $10/5; ◷11am-4pm), a trackless train that departs from Queen Elizabeth II Gate (nearest the Opera House) every half hour for a 25-minute tour.

▶ The park's paths are mostly wheelchair accessible.

▶ You can download self-guided tours from the RBG website.

✕ **Take a Break**

The **Botanic Gardens Restaurant** (Map p30, F4; ☎02-9241 2419; www.trippaswhitegroup.com.au; breakfast $13-16, lunch $32; ◷noon-3pm Mon-Fri, 9.30am-3pm Sat & Sun) is situated within rainforest near the centre of the park.

Attached to the restaurant is a less formal cafe, serving salads, sandwiches, pastries and pastas.

Top Sights
Sydney Harbour Bridge

Whether they're driving over it, climbing up it, jogging across it, shooting fireworks off it or sailing under it, Sydneysiders adore their bridge and swarm around it like ants on ice cream. Dubbed the 'coathanger', it's a spookily big object – moving around town you'll catch sight of it from the corner of your eye, sometimes when you least expect it. Perhaps Sydney poet Kenneth Slessor said it best: 'Day and night, the bridge trembles and echoes like a living thing.'

👁 Map p30, C1

🚉 Circular Quay

BridgeClimb

Don't Miss

The Structure

At 134m high, 1149m long, 49m wide and weighing 53,000 tonnes, the bridge is the largest and heaviest (but not the longest) steel arch in the world. The two halves were built outwards from each shore and were finally bolted together in 1930 after seven years' construction by 1400 workers. It finally opened to the public in 1932.

Pylon Lookout

The bridge's hefty pylons may look as though they're shouldering all the weight, but they're largely decorative – right down to their granite facing. There are awesome views from the top of the **Pylon Lookout** (☎02-9240 1100; www.pylonlookout.com.au; adult/child $13/6.50; ◷10am-5pm; ☒Circular Quay), atop the southeast pylon, 200 steps above the bridge's footpath. Inside the pylon is a small museum.

BridgeClimb

Once only painters and daredevils scaled the bridge. Now, thanks to **BridgeClimb** (☎02-8274 7777; www.bridgeclimb.com; 3 Cumberland St; adult $218-348, child $148-228; ☒Circular Quay), anyone can do it. The scariest part is crossing over the mesh catwalk while under the bridge; on the curved span itself the track is wide enough that you never see straight down.

New Year's Eve

The bridge is the centrepiece of Sydney's major celebrations, particularly the New Year's Eve fireworks. Projections are beamed onto the bridge pylons from around 8pm in the lead-up to the eight-minute Family Fireworks Display at 9pm. Naturally, the main blast sequence is set off on the stroke of midnight.

☑ Top Tips

▶ The best way to experience the bridge is on foot – don't expect much of a view crossing by train or car.

▶ Stairs access the bridge from both shores and a footpath runs along its eastern side.

▶ A pre-BridgeClimb toilet stop is a smart idea; the climb can take up to 3½ hours.

▶ The priciest climbs are at dawn and twilight.

▶ There's only a toll for drivers heading into the city; the other direction is toll-free.

✗ Take a Break

Call into the Harbour View Hotel (p39) for a post-bridge beverage.

At the northern end, **Ripples** (☎02-9929 7722; www.ripplesmilsonspoint.com.au; Olympic Dr, Milsons Point; breakfast $12-18, lunch & dinner $30-38; ◷8am-3pm & 6-11pm; ☒Milsons Point) is an Italian restaurant serving reliable seafood dishes.

A B C D

1

Walsh Bay

Dawes Point

Sydney Harbour Bridge

Dawes Point Park

2

Walsh Bay 27

10

15 Hickson Rd

Lower Fort St

Gedgee St

Campbells Cove

Hickson Rd

DAWES POINT

25

31

11

Windmill Steps

Windmill St 19

Garrison Church 8

Argyle Pl

Trinity Ave

Bradfield Hwy

Cumberland St

Rocks Discovery Museum

33

14

3

17

Argyle St

Watson Rd

Bridge Access Stairs

20

2

Sydney Visitor Centre

34

12 21

MILLERS POINT

Kent St

Argyle La

3

Sydney Observatory

24

THE ROCKS

Susannah Place Museum

5

22

George St

Museum of Contemporary Art

1

Sydney Cove

6 5 4 3 2

Sydney Ferries

4

SH Ervin Gallery

7

Western Distributor

Cumberland St

26

23

Essex St

City Host Information Kiosk

32

Harrington St

First Fleet Park

Cahill Exp

Alfred St

Circular Quay

Customs House

4

Albert

6

Justic & Polic Museu

Gloucester St

Rugby Pl

Pitt St

Reiby Pl

30

35

Grosvenor St

Lang Park

Lang St

Dalley St

Macquarie Place

9

16

Young St

Phillip St

Bridge St

5

Hickson Rd

Jenkins St

Clarence St

Bradfield Hwy

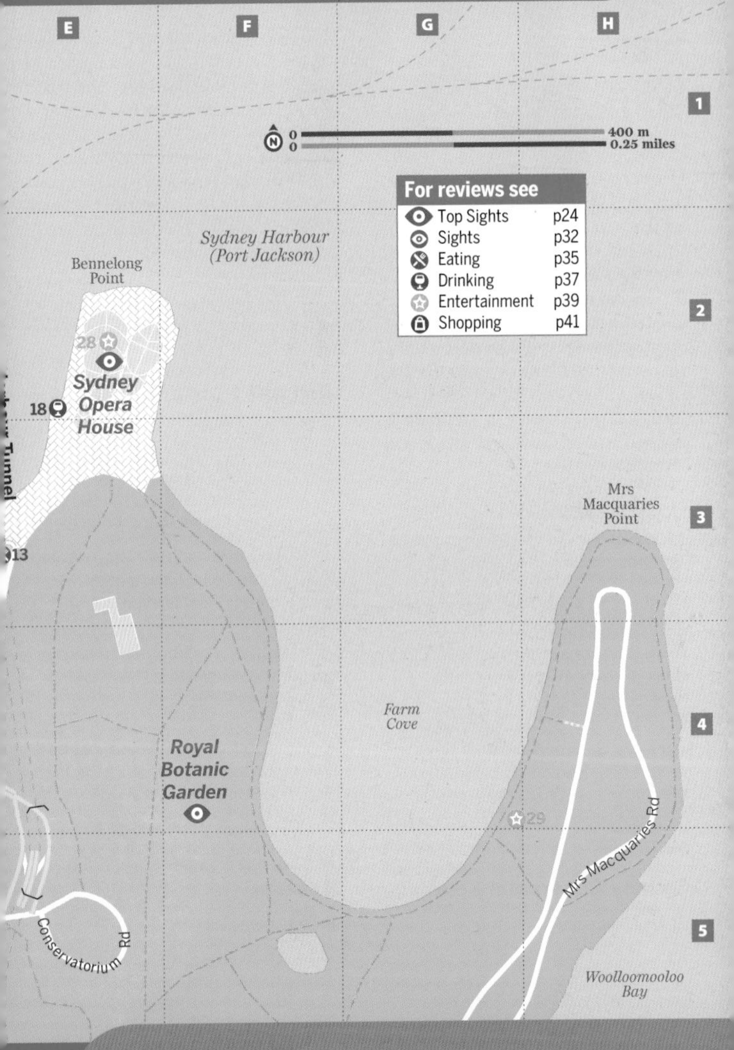

E   F   G   H

1

Ⓝ ⌃ 0 _____ 400 m
       0 _____ 0.25 miles

For reviews see

Ⓞ	Top Sights	p24
⊙	Sights	p32
✕	Eating	p35
🍸	Drinking	p37
⭐	Entertainment	p39
🔒	Shopping	p41

2

Sydney Harbour
(Port Jackson)

Bennelong
Point

28 ⭐
Ⓞ
**Sydney
18 🍸 Opera
House**

Mrs
Macquaries
Point

3

Tunnel

913

Royal
Botanic
Garden
⊙

*Farm
Cove*

4

☆ 29

Mrs Macquaries Rd

5

Conservatorium Rd

*Woolloomooloo
Bay*

Sights

Museum of Contemporary Art
GALLERY

1 ⊙ Map p30, C4

One of country's best and most challenging galleries, the MCA is a showcase for Australian and international contemporary art. Aboriginal art features prominently. The fab Gotham City–style art deco building bears the wounds of a redevelopment that has grafted on additional gallery space and a rooftop cafe/sculpture terrace – and ruined the George St facade in the process. (☑02-9245 2400; www.mca.com.au; 140 George St; admission free; ⊙10am-5pm Fri-Wed, to 9pm Thu; ⍰Circular Quay)

Rocks Discovery Museum
MUSEUM

2 ⊙ Map p30, C3

Divided into four chronological displays – Warrane (pre-1788), Colony (1788–1820), Port (1820–1900) and Transformations (1900 to the present) – this excellent museum digs deep into the Rocks' history and leads you on an artefact-rich tour. Sensitive attention is given to the Rocks' original inhabitants, the Gadigal people. (☑02-9240 8680; www. rocksdiscoverymuseum.com; Kendall Lane; admission free; ⊙10am-5pm; ⍰Circular Quay)

Sydney Observatory
OBSERVATORY

3 ⊙ Map p30, A3

Built in the 1850s, Sydney's copper-domed, Italianate observatory squats atop pretty **Observatory Hill**, overlooking the harbour. Inside is a collection of vintage apparatus, including Australia's oldest working telescope (1874). Also on offer are audiovisual displays, including Aboriginal sky stories and a virtual reality **3D Theatre** (www.sydneyobservatory. au; adult/child $10/8; ⊙2.30pm & 3.30pm daily, plus 11am & noon Sat & Sun; ⍰Circular Quay). Bookings are essential for night-time stargazing sessions (adult/child $18/12). (☑02-9921 3485; www.sydneyobservatory.com. au; 1003 Upper Fort St; admission free; ⊙10am-5pm; ⍰Circular Quay)

Customs House
HISTORIC BUILDING

4 ⊙ Map p30, D4

This elegant harbourside edifice (1885) houses a bar, Cafe Sydney (p36), on the top floor, and the three-level **Customs House Library** (☑02-9242 8555; 31 Alfred St; ⊙10am-7pm Mon-Fri, 11am-4pm Sat & Sun; ⍰Circular Quay), which has a great selection of international newspapers and magazines, internet access and interesting temporary exhibitions. In the lobby, look for the swastikas in the tiling (and the plaque explaining their symbolism), and a fascinating 1:500 model of the inner city under the glass floor. (☑02-9242 8555; www.sydneycustomshouse.com.au; 31 Alfred St; admission free; ⊙10am-7pm Mon-Fri, 11am-4pm Sat & Sun; ⍰Circular Quay)

Susannah Place Museum
MUSEUM

5 ⊙ Map p30, B4

Dating from 1844, this diminutive terrace of four houses and a shop

Understand
Colonial Beginnings

When the American War of Independence disrupted the transportation of convicts to North America, Britain lost its main dumping ground for undesirables and needed somewhere else to put them. Joseph Banks, who had been Lieutenant James Cook's scientific leader during the expedition to Australia in 1770, piped up with the suggestion that Botany Bay would be a fine new site for criminals.

First Fleet
The 11 ships of the First Fleet landed at Botany Bay in January 1788 – a motley crew of 730 male and female convicts, 400 sailors, four companies of marines, and enough livestock and booze to last two years. Captain Arthur Phillip quickly rejected Botany Bay as a suitable site for a settlement and sailed 25km north to the harbour Cook had named Port Jackson, where he discovered a crucial source of fresh water in what he called Sydney Cove (today's Circular Quay). The day was 26 January 1788, now celebrated as Australia Day. Conversely, many Aboriginal people refer to it as 'Invasion Day' or 'Survival Day'.

The Disreputable Rocks
The socioeconomic divide of the future city was foreshadowed when the convicts were allocated the rocky land to the west of the stream (known unimaginatively as the Rocks), while the governor and other officials pitched their tents to the east.

Built with convict labour between 1837 and 1844, Circular Quay was originally (and more accurately) called Semi-circular Quay, and acted as the main port of Sydney. In the 1850s it was extended further, covering over the by-then festering Tank Stream, which ran through the middle.

As time went on, whalers and sailors joined the ex-convicts at the Rocks – and inns and brothels sprang up to entertain them. With the settlement filthy and overcrowded, the nouveau riche started building houses on the upper slopes, their sewage flowing to the slums below. Bubonic plague broke out in 1900, leading to the razing of entire streets, while the Harbour Bridge's construction in the 1920s wiped out even more. It wasn't until the 1970s that the Rocks' cultural and architectural heritage was finally recognised.

selling historical wares is a fascinating time capsule of life in the Rocks since colonial times. After you watch a short film about the people who lived here, a guide will take you through the claustrophobic homes, which are decorated to reflect different periods in their histories. (☏02-9241 1893; www.sydneylivingmuseums.com.au; 58-64 Gloucester St; adult/child $8/4; ⏱tours 2pm, 3pm & 4pm; �🚉Circular Quay)

Justice & Police Museum

MUSEUM

6 ◎ Map p30, D4

Occupying the old Water Police Station (1858), this mildly unnerving museum documents the city's dark and disreputable past through old police photographs and an often macabre collection of exhibits. (☏02-9252 1144; www.sydneylivingmuseums.com.au; cnr Albert & Phillip Sts; adult/child $10/5; ⏱10am-5pm Sat & Sun; 🚉Circular Quay)

SH Ervin Gallery

GALLERY

7 ◎ Map p30, A4

High on the hill inside the old Fort St School (1856), the SH Ervin Gallery exhibits invariably rewarding historical and contemporary Australian art. Annual mainstays include the Salon des Refusés (alternative Archibald Prize entries) and the Portia Geach Memorial Award. There's a cafe here, too. (☏02-9258 0173; www.shervingallery.com.au; Watson Rd; adult/concession/under 12 $7/5/free; ⏱11am-5pm Tue-Sun; 🚉Wynyard)

Garrison Church

CHURCH

8 ◎ Map p30, B3

Also known as Holy Trinity (1843), this chunky sandstone Anglican church on the western side of the Argyle Cut was the colony's first military church. Below a dark timber ceiling, the hushed interior is spangled with dusty, lank-hanging regimental flags. Australia's first prime minister, Edmund Barton, went to school here (the parish hall doubled as a schoolhouse). (☏02-9247 1268; www.thegarrisonchurch.org.au; 62 Lower Fort St; ⏱9am-5pm; 🚉Circular Quay)

Macquarie Place

SQUARE

9 ◎ Map p30, C5

Beneath some shady Moreton Bay fig trees a block or two back from the Quay is this little historic triangle. Look for the actual **cannon and anchor** from the First Fleet flagship (HMS *Sirius*), an ornate but defunct 1857 drinking fountain, a National Trust–classified gentlemen's *pissoir* (closed) and an 1818 **obelisk** erected 'to record that all the public roads leading to the interior of the colony are measured from it'.

The park is overlooked by the imposing 19th-century **Lands Department Building**; the north facade bears statues of Sturt, Hume, Leichhardt and other early Australian movers and shakers. (cnr Loftus & Bridge Sts; 🚉Circular Quay)

Walsh Bay

WATERFRONT

10 ◎ Map p30, B2

This section of Dawes Point waterfront was Sydney's busiest before the advent

Understand

Bennelong

Bennelong was born around 1764 into the Wangal tribe, who lived around Glebe. In 1789 he was kidnapped on the orders of Governor Arthur Phillip, who hoped to use the captive to learn the customs and language of the reclusive locals. Eventually he escaped, but returned by 1791 when reassured that he would not be held against his will. He learnt to speak English and developed a friendship with Governor Phillip, who had a brick hut built for him on what is now Bennelong Point, where the Sydney Opera House stands.

In 1792 Bennelong went on a 'civilising' trip to England, and returned in 1795 with a changed dress sense and altered behaviour. Described as good-natured and 'stoutly made', Bennelong ultimately was no longer accepted by Aboriginal society and never really found happiness with the colonists either. He died a broken, dispossessed man in 1813, possibly as a result of his affection for the bottle.

of container shipping and the construction of new port facilities at Botany Bay. The last decade has seen the Federation-era wharves here gentrified beyond belief, morphing into luxury hotels, apartments, theatre spaces, power-boat marinas and restaurants.

The self-guided 1.6km Walsh Bay Walk starts at Pier 2 and leads you through 11 stops, with interesting plaques and directions urging you onwards; download a guide from the Walsh Bay website. Pier 4 houses the Wharf Theatre, home to the renowned Sydney Theatre Company, Sydney Dance Company and Bangarra Dance Theatre. (www.walshbaysydney.com.au; Hickson Rd; ⌂Wynyard)

Eating

Quay
MODERN AUSTRALIAN $$$

11 Map p30, C3

Quay is shamelessly guilty of breaking the rule that good views make for bad food. Chef Peter Gilmore never rests on his laurels, consistently delivering the exquisitely crafted, adventurous cuisine which has landed Quay on the prestigious World's Best Restaurants list. And the view? Like dining in a postcard. (☎02-9251 5600; www.quay.com.au; L3, Overseas Passenger Terminal; 3/4 courses $130/150; ◷noon-2.30pm Tue-Fri, 6-10pm daily; ⌂Circular Quay)

Saké

12   Map p30, B3   JAPANESE $$$

Colourful sake barrels and lots of dark wood contribute to the louche Oriental glamour of this large, buzzy restaurant. Solo travellers can prop themselves around the open kitchen and snack on delectable Wagyu dumplings and maki rolls, while couples tuck into multicourse banquets of contemporary Japanese cuisine (from $88). (☏02-9259 5656; www.sakerestaurant.com.au; 12 Argyle St; mains $25-45; ⏱noon-3pm & 5.30-10.30pm; ☒Circular Quay)

Aria

13   Map p30, E3   MODERN AUSTRALIAN $$$

Aria is a star in Sydney's fine-dining firmament, an award-winning combination of chef Matt Moran's stellar dishes, Opera House views and faultless service. A pretheatre à la carte menu is available before 7pm. (☏02-9240 2255; www.ariarestaurant.com; 1 Macquarie St; lunch & pretheatre mains $46, 2-/3-/4-course dinner $105/130/155; ⏱noon-2.30pm Mon-Fri, 5.30-11pm daily; ☒Circular Quay)

Cafe Sydney

MODERN AUSTRALIAN $$$

This breezy, spacious restaurant on the Customs House roof (see 4 ◉ Map p30, D4) has harbour views, an outdoor terrace, a glass ceiling, a cocktail bar and friendly staff. Seafood dishes dominate. (☏02-9251 8683; www.cafe sydney.com; L5, Customs House, 31 Alfred St; mains $38-39; ⏱noon-11pm Mon-Fri, 5-11pm Sat, noon-3.30pm Sun; ☒Circular Quay)

Sailors Thai Canteen

14   Map p30, C3   THAI $$

Wedge yourself into a gap between arts-community operators, politicians and media manoeuvrers at Sailors' long communal table and order from the fragrant menu of Thai street-food classics. The balcony tables fill up fast, but fortune might be smiling on you. Downstairs the vibe's more formal and the prices higher. (☏02-9251 2466; www.sailorsthai.com.au; 106 George St; mains $24-29; ⏱noon-3pm Mon-Fri & 5-10pm daily; ☒Circular Quay)

Cafe Sopra

15   Map p30, B2   ITALIAN $$

Branches of this acclaimed Italian restaurant, paired with the associated Fratelli Fresh providore, have been popping up all over town. This one's easily the best place to eat in Walsh Bay. (www.fratellifresh.com.au; 16 Hickson Rd; mains $20-30; ⏱noon-3pm & 6-10pm; ☒Wynyard)

Tramezzini Espresso

16   Map p30, D5   CAFE $

There aren't a lot of decent downtown places for a reasonably priced, healthy bite, so this Italian cafe in the foyer of the AMP building is worth remembering. Unsurprisingly, the clientele is extremely suity, but don't let that and all the ostentatious marble get in the way of a flat white and a zingy egg-and-parmesan breakfast roll. (☏02-9232 0422; 50 Bridge St; mains $4-8; ⏱6.30am-5pm Mon-Fri; ☒Circular Quay)

Opera Bar

Drinking

Lord Nelson Brewery Hotel
PUB, BREWERY

 17 Map p30, A3

Built in 1836 and converted into a pub in 1841, this atmospheric sandstone boozer is one of three claiming to be Sydney's oldest (all using slightly different criteria). The on-site brewery cooks up its own natural ales (try the Old Admiral). (02-9251 4044; 19 Kent St; 11am-11pm; Circular Quay)

Opera Bar
BAR, LIVE MUSIC

18 Map p30, E2

Right on the harbour with the Opera House on one side and the Harbour Bridge on the other, this perfectly positioned terrace manages a very Sydney marriage of the laid-back and the sophisticated. A recent takeover by celebrity chef Matt Moran has shifted the food up a notch. There's live music or DJs most nights. (www.operabar.com. au; lower concourse, Sydney Opera House; 11.30am-midnight Mon-Fri, 9am-midnight Sat & Sun; Circular Quay)

Hero of Waterloo
PUB

19 🍺 Map p30, B3

Enter this rough-hewn 1843 sandstone pub to meet some locals, chat up the Irish bar staff and grab an earful of the swing, folk and Celtic bands (Friday to Sunday). Downstairs is a dungeon where, in days gone by, drinkers would sleep off a heavy night before being shanghaied to the high seas via a tunnel leading straight to the harbour. (www.heroofwaterloo.com.au; 81 Lower Fort St; ⏰10am-11pm; ⓡCircular Quay)

Glenmore at the Rocks
PUB

20 🍺 Map p30, B3

Downstairs it's a predictably nice old Rocks pub, but head up to the rooftop and the views are beyond fabulous: Opera House, harbour and city skyline all present and accounted for. It gets rammed up here on the weekends, with DJs, good food and plenty of wine by the glass. (www.theglenmore.com.au; 96 Cumberland St; ⏰11am-midnight; 📶; ⓡCircular Quay)

Argyle
BAR

21 🍺 Map p30, B3

This mammoth conglomeration of five bars is spread through the historic sandstone Argyle Stores buildings, including a cobblestone courtyard and underground cellars resonating with DJ beats. The decor ranges from rococo couches to white extruded plastic tables, all offset with kooky chandeliers and moody lighting. Great bar food, too. (☎02-9247 5500; www.theargylerocks.com; 18 Argyle St; ⏰11am-midnight Sun-Wed, to 3am Thu-Sat; ⓡCircular Quay)

Fortune of War
PUB

22 🍺 Map p30, C4

This 1828 drinking den retains much of its original charm and, by the looks of things, some of the original punters, too. There's live music on Thursday, Friday and Saturday nights and on weekend afternoons. (www.fortuneofwar.com.au; 137 George St; ⏰9am-midnight Sun-Thu, to 3am Fri & Sat; ⓡCircular Quay)

Harts Pub
PUB

23 🍺 Map p30, B4

Pouring a range of craft beers, Harts is frequented by locals drawn by the beer, the rugby tipping competition and some of Sydney's best pub food. (www.hartspub.com; cnr Essex & Gloucester Sts; ⏰noon-midnight; ⓡCircular Quay)

Australian Hotel
PUB

24 🍺 Map p30, B3

Not only is this pub architecturally notable (c1913), it also boasts a bonza selection of fair dinkum Ocker (local) beer and wine. Keeping with the antipodean theme, the kitchen fires up pizzas topped with kangaroo and saltwater crocodile ($17 to $27). (www.australianheritagehotel.com; 100 Cumberland St; ⏰11am-midnight; ⓡCircular Quay)

Harbour View Hotel

PUB

25 🚇 Map p30, B2

Built in the 1920s, the curvilicious Harbour View was the main boozer for the Harbour Bridge construction crew. These days it fulfils the same duties for the BridgeClimbers – wave to them from the 2nd-floor balcony as they traverse the lofty girders. The Tooth's KB Lager listed on the tiles out the front is long gone, but there's plenty of Heineken and James Squire on tap. (📞02-9252 4111; www.harbourview. com.au; 18 Lower Fort St; ⏰11am-midnight Mon-Sat, to 10pm Sun; 🛜; 🚉Circular Quay)

Blu Bar on 36

COCKTAIL BAR

26 🚇 Map p30, B4

The drinks may be pricey, but it's well worth heading up to the top of the Shangri-La hotel for the views, which seem to stretch all the way to New Zealand. The dress code is officially 'smart casual', but err on the side of smart if you can't handle rejection. (www.shangri-la.com; Level 36, 176 Cumberland St; ⏰5pm-midnight; 🚉Circular Quay)

Entertainment

Sydney Theatre Company

THEATRE

27 ⭐ Map p30, B2

Established in 1978, the STC is Sydney theatre's top dog and has played an important part in the careers of many

famous Australian actors (especially Cate Blanchett, who was co-artistic director from 2008 to 2013). Tours of the company's Wharf and Roslyn Packer theatres are held at 10.30am every Tuesday ($10). Performances are also staged at the Opera House. (STC; 📞02-9250 1777; www.sydneytheatre.com.au; Pier 4/5, 15 Hickson Rd; ⏰box office 9am-8.30pm Mon-Fri, 11am-8.30pm Sat, 2hr before show Sun; 🚉Wynyard)

Opera Australia

OPERA

28 ⭐ Map p30, E2

Opera Australia is the big player in Oz opera, staging over 600 performances a year. The company's Sydney shows are performed in the Opera House, unless they're staging a big outdoor extravaganza on the harbour or in the Domain. (📞02-9318 8200; www.opera-australia.org.au; Sydney Opera House; tickets $49-199; 🚉Circular Quay)

Bangarra Dance Theatre   DANCE

Bangarra (see 27 ⊕ Map p30, B2) is hailed as Australia's finest Aboriginal performance company. Artistic director Stephen Page conjures a fusion of contemporary themes, Indigenous traditions and Western technique. When not touring internationally, the company performs at the Opera House or at their own small theatre in Walsh Bay. (☏02-9251 5333; www. bangarra.com.au; Pier 4/5, 15 Hickson Rd; tickets $30-93; ⓡWynyard)

Sydney Dance Company   DANCE

Australia's number-one contemporary-dance company has been staging wildly modern, sexy, sometimes shocking works for nearly 40 years. Performances are usually held across the street at the Sydney Theatre Company's (see 27 ⊕ Map p30, B2) Roslyn Packer Theatre, or at Carriageworks. (SDC; ☏02-9221 4811; www. sydneydancecompany.com; Pier 4/5, 15 Hickson Rd; ⓡWynyard)

Australian Ballet   DANCE

The Melbourne-based Australian Ballet performs a wide repertoire of classical as well as contemporary works. See them twinkle their toes at the Opera House or the Capitol Theatre. (☏1300 369 741; www.australianballet.com.au; tickets $39-289)

Sydney Symphony Orchestra   CLASSICAL MUSIC

The SSO plays around 150 concerts annually with famous local and international musicians. Catch them at the Sydney Opera House or the City Recital Hall. (☏02-8215 4600; www. sydneysymphony.com)

Australian Chamber Orchestra   CLASSICAL MUSIC

Since 1975 the ACO has been making chamber music sexy and adventurous, especially under the tutelage of artistic director and lead violinist Richard Tognetti. Concerts are staged throughout the year at the Opera House and City Recital Hall. (☏02-8274 3888; www. aco.com.au; tickets $46-127)

Bell Shakespeare   THEATRE

Australia's Shakespeare specialists stage their Sydney performances in the Opera House. Their repertoire occasionally deviates from the bard to the likes of Marlowe and Molière. (☏02-8298 9000; www.bellshakespeare.com. au; tickets $75-79)

OpenAir Cinema   CINEMA

29 ⭐   Map p30, G4

Right on the harbour, the outdoor three-storey screen here comes with surround sound, sunsets, skyline and swanky food and wine. Most tickets are purchased in advance, but a limited number of tickets go on sale at the door each night at 6.30pm; check the website for details. (www.stgeorge openair.com.au; Mrs Macquaries Rd; tickets $37; ⊗Jan & Feb; ⓡCircular Quay)

Basement

LIVE MUSIC

30 ⭐ Map p30, C5

Once solely a jazz venue, the Basement now hosts international and local musicians working in many disciplines and genres. Dinner-and-show tickets net you a table by the stage, guaranteeing a better view than the standing-only area by the bar. (☏02-9251 2797; www.thebasement.com.au; 7 Macquarie Pl; admission $8-60; ☒Circular Quay)

Shopping

The Rocks Markets

MARKET

31 🔒 Map p30, C3

Under a long white canopy, the 150 stalls at this weekend market are a little on the tacky side, but there are some gems to be uncovered. The Friday 'Foodies Market' is more fulfilling (and filling). (www.therocksmarket.com; George St; ☺9am-3pm Fri, 10am-5pm Sat & Sun; ☒Circular Quay)

Australian Wine Centre

WINE

32 🔒 Map p30, C4

This multilingual basement store is packed with quality Australian wine, beer and spirits. Smaller producers are well represented, along with a staggering range of prestigious Penfolds Grange wines. International shipping can be arranged. (www.australianwinecentre.com; Goldfields House, 1 Alfred St; ☺10am-8pm Mon-Sat, to 6.30pm Sun; ☒Circular Quay)

Opal Minded

JEWELLERY

33 🔒 Map p30, C3

As good a place as any to stock up on that quintessential piece of Aussie bling. (www.opalminded.com; 55 George St; ☺9am-6.30pm; ☒Circular Quay)

Gannon House

ART

34 🔒 Map p30, C3

Specialising in contemporary Australian and Aboriginal art, Gannon House purchases works directly from artists and Aboriginal communities. You'll find the work of prominent artists such as Gloria Petyarre here, alongside lesser-known names. (☏02-9251 4474; www.gannonhousegallery.com; 45 Argyle St; ☒Circular Quay)

Herringbone

CLOTHING

35 🔒 Map p30, C5

Branch of the Sydney shirt company, whose products combine Australian design and Italian fabrics. (www.herringbone.com; 7 Macquarie Pl; ☺9am-6pm Mon-Wed & Fri, to 8pm Thu, 10am-5pm Sat, 11am-4pm Sun; ☒Circular Quay)

Local Life
A Journey up the Parramatta River

Getting There

⚓ Catch the ferry from Circular Quay to Balmain East (Darling St). The cheapest option is to use an Opal smartcard, which is capped at $15 per day.

Sydney Harbour gets all the attention but a jaunt upriver is just as interesting. As you pass old industrial sites and gaze into millionaires' back-yards, a window opens onto a watery world in the heart of Sydney where school rowing crews get put through their paces, groups of mates glide past on yachts and solo kayakers work up a sweat.

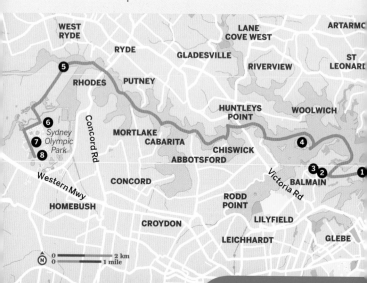

❶ Wander Through Balmain

Balmain is home to dozens of histori-cally significant buildings. As you head up Darling St look for **Waterman's Cottage** (1841) at No 12; **Cathermore** (1841), Balmain's first bakery, which later became the Waterford Arms pub, at No 50; and the **Watch House** (1854), Sydney's oldest surviving lock-up, at No 179.

❷ Adriano Zumbo Patisserie

Australia's highest-profile pastry chef introduced the nation to macarons during a stint on TV's *MasterChef*. Call into his **patisserie** (www.adrianozumbo. com; 296 Darling St, Balmain; sweets $2.50-10; ☺8am-6pm; 🚢Balmain) to stock up on 'zumbarons', tarts and cakes as astonishing to look at as they are to eat.

❸ Rock the Kazbah

Balmain's best restaurant, **Kazbah** (☎02-9555 7067; www.kazbah.com.au; 379 Darling St, Balmain; breakfast $12-23, lunch $19-29, dinner $28-34; ☺8am-3pm Sat & Sun, 11.30am-3pm Tue-Fri, 5.30-9.30pm Tue-Sat; 🚢Balmain) is an Aladdin's cave filled with Moorish decorations and the flavours of the Maghreb.

❹ Explore Cockatoo Island

Catch a ferry from Balmain to Cockatoo Island, where the harbour and river meet. A tunnel passes clear through the island and you can explore the remains of a convict-era prison and shipyard.

❺ Cycle Sydney Olympic Park

Continue by ferry to 640-hectare Sydney Olympic Park. It incorporates na-ture reserves and 35km of cycleways. The best way to explore is by bike (www.bikehiresydneyolympic park.com.au); on weekends and school holidays you can also hire one from Blaxland Riverside Park, 1.5km west along the river from the ferry wharf.

❻ Take the Brickpit Ring Walk

This brightly coloured circular **walkway** (Australia Ave; admission free; ☺sunrise-sunset; 🚉Olympic Park), an Olympic Park attraction, sits 18m above an aban-doned brickworks on what looks like metal chopsticks. Three billion bricks were made here between 1911 and 1988. Built into the loop are multimedia ex-hibits about the brick workers and the area's rare amphibious inhabitants.

❼ Check out ANZ Stadium

The main Olympic venues are 3km from the wharf, so you're best to cycle. **ANZ Stadium** (☎02-8765 2300; www.anzstadium. com.au; Olympic Blvd; tours adult/child $29/19; ☺tours 11am, 1pm & 3pm daily, gantry 9am Fri-Wed; 🚉Olympic Park) is an imposing oval bedpan with a colourful sculpture of na-tive feathers spiralling over its entrance.

❽ Dive into the Aquatic Centre

Indulge your Ian Thorpe or Misty Hyman fantasies in the actual record-shattering **pool** (☎02-9752 3666; www. aquaticcentre.com.au; Olympic Blvd; adult/child $7/6; ☺5am-9pm Mon-Fri, 6am-7pm Sat & Sun; 🚉Olympic Park) that was used in the 2000 Olympics. It also has a leisure pool with a whirlpool in one corner, a state-of-the-art gym, a cafe and a swim shop.

Top Sights
Taronga Zoo

Getting There

Taronga Zoo is located in Mosman on the North Shore, roughly halfway between Circular Quay and Manly.

⛴ Ferries from Circular Quay depart every half an hour.

A day trip to Taronga offers so much more than the zoo itself: running the gauntlet of didgeridoo players and living statues at Circular Quay; the ferry ride past the Opera House and out into the harbour; the cable car from the wharf to the top gate; the ever-present views of the city skyline as you make your way down through 75 hectares of bushy harbour hillside. And to cap it all off, the enclosures are excellent, too.

Sydney skyline from Taronga Zoo

Don't Miss

Australian Natives

As you'd expect, Taronga Zoo is chock-full of kangaroos, koalas and similarly hirsute Australian creatures. The zoo's 4000 critters have million-dollar harbour views but seem blissfully unaware of the privilege. The animals are well looked after, with more natural open enclosures than cages. Highlights include the nocturnal platypus habitat and the Great Southern Oceans section.

Talks & Encounters

Throughout the day there are over 20 keeper-led feedings, educational talks and demonstrations. One of the highlights is the free-flight bird show at midday and 3pm, where remarkably tame raptors and parrots swoop over an open-air amphitheatre facing the harbour. Equally popular is the seal show, featuring Australian and Californian sea lions and New Zealand fur seals.

Tours

Tours include **Nura Diya** (www.taronga.org.au; 90min tour adult/child $99/69; ⊘9.45am Mon, Wed & Fri), where Indigenous guides introduce you to native animals and share Dreaming stories about them, while giving an insight into traditional Aboriginal life. The **Wild Australia Experience** (adult/child $127/81) is a small group tour with a keeper that allows hands-on contact with the animals.

Roar & Snore Sleepover

Roar & Snore (☑02-9978 4791; www.taronga.org.au; adult/child $320/205) is an overnight family experience that includes a night-time safari, a buffet dinner, breakfast and tents under the stars.

☑02-9969 2777

www.taronga.org.au

Bradleys Head Rd

adult/child $46/23

⊘9.30am-5pm

⚏Taronga Zoo

☑ Top Tips

▸ A **Zoo Pass** (adult/child/family $51/25/143) from Circular Quay includes return ferry rides, the bus or cable car ride to the top and zoo admission.

▸ The ferry ride takes 12 minutes.

▸ Parking is scarce – take public transport instead.

▸ Disabled access is good, even if arriving by ferry, and wheelchairs are available.

✗ Take a Break

Acclaimed Italian chef Giovanni Pilu runs the **Taronga Piazza** cafe, just inside the main entrance.

The zoo's main restaurant is the **View**, which overlooks the harbour. There's also a bakery cafe, takeaway kiosks and picnic areas scattered about the grounds.

Explore

City Centre & Haymarket

Before suburban sprawl started in earnest in the mid-19th century, this area (along with the Rocks) *was* Sydney. Today it's a towering central business district (CBD) – Australia's economic engine room – with skyscrapers shadowing sandstone colonial buildings and churches. The breathless jumble of Haymarket and Chinatown provides the yin to the CBD's yang.

The Sights in a Day

Spend most of the morning exploring the **Art Gallery of NSW** (p48), then stroll through the Domain to **St Mary's Cathedral** (p54). Cross into Hyde Park and head straight through its centre, crossing Park St and continuing on to the **Anzac Memorial** (p55). Pop down to Chinatown for lunch; **Mamak** (p58) is an excellent option.

Explore **Chinatown** (p55): wander through Dixon St and into **Paddy's Markets** (p67). Head back along George St to the **Town Hall** (p57) and **Queen Victoria Building** (p65). If the shopping bug bites, continue on to Sydney's main shopping strip, Pitt St Mall, in the shadow of **Sydney Tower** (p56). Once you're all shopped out, spend the rest of your afternoon at the **Museum of Sydney** (p56).

Get in early to score a table at **Mr Wong** (p57) and then seek out some of the city's tucked-away bars; **Frankie's Pizza** (p60) and **Baxter Inn** (p60) are our favourites. If you're not ready to call it a night, check out what's going down at **Good God Small Club** (p62).

For a local's day in the City Centre & Haymarket, see p50.

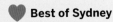

Top Sights

Art Gallery of NSW (p48)

Local Life

City Escapes (p50)

Best of Sydney

Eating

Tetsuya's (p57)

Rockpool (p57)

Mr Wong (p57)

Spice Temple (p58)

Drinking

Baxter Inn (p60)

Grandma's (p60)

O Bar (p62)

Getting There

Train By far the best option for getting here, with stations at Central, Town Hall, Wynyard, Martin Place, St James and Museum.

Bus Numerous bus routes traverse the city centre. Railway Sq is a major hub.

Light Rail City stops include Central, Capitol Square and Paddy's Markets; a handy option if you're coming from Glebe or Pyrmont.

Top Sights
Art Gallery of NSW

With its classical Greek frontage and modern rear end, the Art Gallery of NSW plays a prominent and gregarious role in Sydney society. Blockbuster international touring exhibitions arrive regularly and there's an outstanding permanent collection of Australian art, including a substantial Indigenous collection. The gallery also plays host to a lively line-up of lectures, concerts, screenings, celebrity talks and children's activities.

◉ Map p52, E3

☎ 1800 679 278

www.artgallery.nsw.gov.au

Art Gallery Rd

admission free

🕑 10am-5pm Thu-Tue, to 10pm Wed

🚇 St James

Don't Miss

Australian Collections

As you enter, the galleries to the left are devoted to 20th- and 21st-century Australian works (featuring the likes of Sidney Nolan, Grace Cossington Smith and James Gleeson), while to the right the central room contains local 19th-century art (including Arthur Streeton's 1891 work, *Fire's On*). In the entrance court in the middle, look out for *The Balcony 2* (1975), Brett Whiteley's luminous depiction of Sydney Harbour.

An absolute highlight is the Yiribana Gallery on the lowest level, containing a wonderful Aboriginal and Torres Strait Islander collection (including works by Binyinyuwuy, Tom Djawa and Brenda L Croft).

European Collection

Also on the ground floor, the European art collection is split into two sections: 15th to 19th century (Constable, Gainsborough, Rubens) and 19th and 20th century (Degas, Van Gogh, Monet, Rodin).

Asian Collection

Ceramics and religious art from the gallery's well-regarded Asian collection are displayed at the rear of the ground level. The remainder of the collection (Chinese, Korean and Japanese art) is on the first of the lower levels, by the cafe.

Lower Level 2

Lower level 2 has the constantly changing contemporary (Gilbert & George, Jeff Koons, Sol LeWitt) and photography galleries. In the Modern Gallery, look out for Pablo Picasso's *Nude in a Rocking Chair* (1956) and Antony Gormley's sculpture *Haft* (2007).

☑ Top Tips

▶ A range of free guided tours is offered on different themes and in various languages; enquire at the desk or check the website.

▶ The gallery's most famous annual show features entries in the unfailingly controversial Archibald Prize for portraiture, Wynne Prize for landscape painting or figure sculpture and Sulman Prize for subject or mural painting (usually held between July and September; admission $12).

▶ Junior art lovers can follow tailored trails, and attend free performances (2.30pm Sundays).

✗ Take a Break

Matt Moran's excellent **Chiswick at the Gallery restaurant** (☏ 02-9225 1819; www.chiswickrestaurant.com.au; Art Gallery Rd; weekday mains $27-35, weekend $32-38; ◷ noon-3.30pm Thu-Tue, to 9pm Wed; ⊠ St James) is located at the rear of the entrance level.

There's a more informal cafe on the floor below.

Local Life
City Escapes

Sydney's two most imposing streets are Macquarie St, the centre of government, and intersecting with it, Martin Place, its financial heart. During weekdays they thrum to the beat of politics and commerce. When the daily hustle gets too much, bureaucrats and office workers seek sanctuary in the inner city's parks or head to Pitt Street Mall for some shopfront fantasies.

1 Dawdle through the Domain

This **large grassy tract** (www.rbgsyd.nsw. gov.au; Art Gallery Rd; ⊞St James) was set aside by Governor Phillip in 1788 for public recreation. Today's city workers use the space to work up a sweat or eat their lunch. Large-scale public events are also held here. Speakers' Corner, on the lawn in front of the Art Gallery, attracts all manner of engaging and enraging orators.

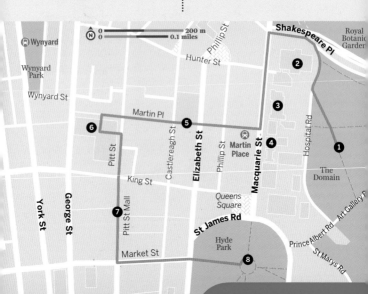

② Study the State Library

Scholars sneak off to the elegant main reading room of the **State Library of NSW** (☎02-9273 1414; www.sl.nsw.gov.au; Macquarie St; admission free; ⊙9am-8pm Mon-Thu, 10am-5pm Fri-Sun; ⬚Martin Place) seeking inspiration within its milky marble walls. The library holds more than five million tomes, including James Cook's and Joseph Banks' journals. Drop in to peruse the temporary exhibitions.

③ Visit the People's Place

Built in 1816 as part of the Rum Hospital, **Parliament House** (☎02-9230 2111; www.parliament.nsw.gov.au; 6 Macquarie St; admission free; ⊙9am-5pm Mon-Fri; ⬚Martin Place) has been home to the Parliament of New South Wales since 1829, making it the world's oldest continually operating parliament building. Everyone's welcome to visit the assembly chambers, art exhibitions and historical displays.

④ Sydney Hospital

Australia's oldest **hospital** (☎02-9382 7111; www.seslhd.health.nsw.gov.au/SHSEH; 8 Macquarie St; ⬚Martin Place) has a grand Victorian sandstone facade and a peaceful central courtyard with a cafe and a kitsch enamelled swan fountain. In provocative recline out the front of the hospital is the pig-ugly bronze statue *Il Porcellino*. Rub its snout for luck.

⑤ March down Martin Place

Studded with imposing edifices, long, lean Martin Place was closed to traffic in 1971, forming a terraced pedestrian mall. It's the closest thing to a town square that Sydney has. Once the corporate crowds go home, skateboarders converge upon the ramps, stairs and fountains. Near the George St end is the Cenotaph, commemorating Australia's war dead.

⑥ Rehydrate in GPO Sydney

As iconic as the Opera House in its time (1874), this colonnaded Victorian palazzo has been gutted, stabbed with office towers and transformed into a Westin hotel, swanky shops, restaurants and bars. Under a staircase in the basement there is a small historical display and a pipe housing the dribbling remnants of the Tank Stream.

⑦ Pitt Street Mall Shopping

Sydneysiders head to Pitt Street Mall when they've got something special to buy or when some serious retail therapy is required. As you sidestep the buskers on this car-free thoroughfare, look out for the Strand Arcade on your right and Westfield Sydney on your left.

⑧ Hang out in Hyde Park

Formal but much-loved Hyde Park has manicured gardens and a tree-formed tunnel running down its spine, which looks particularly pretty at night when illuminated by fairy lights. The park's northern end is crowned by the richly symbolic art deco Archibald Memorial Fountain, featuring Greek mythological figures, while at the other end is the Anzac Memorial.

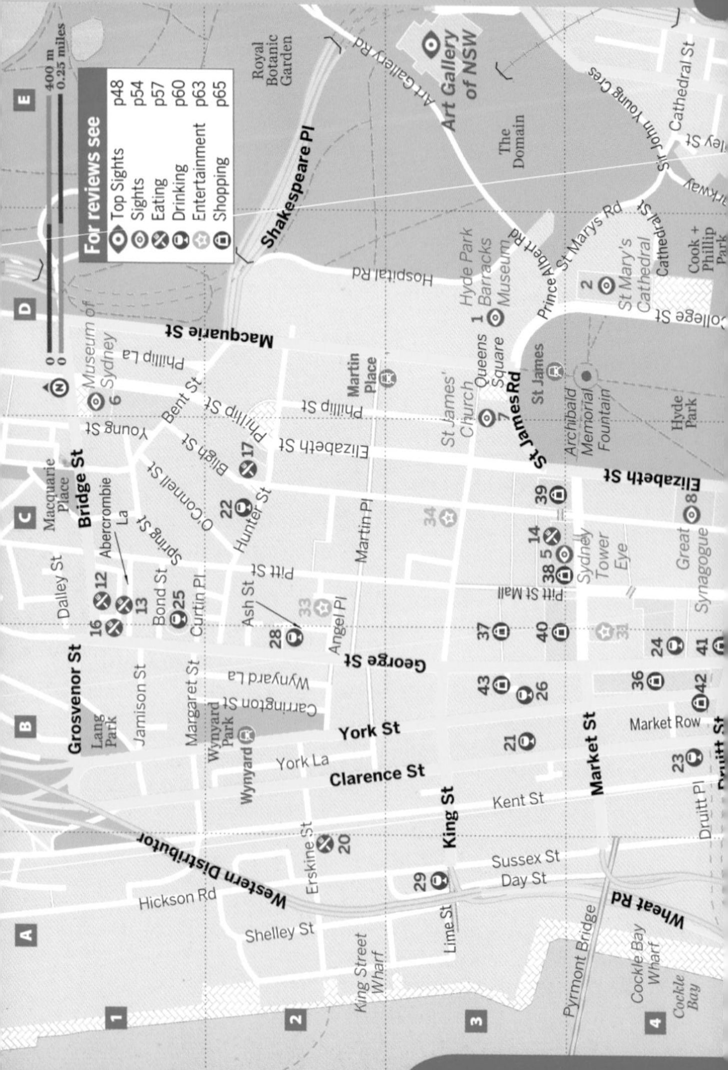

For reviews see
Top Sights p48
Sights p54
Eating p57
Drinking p60
Entertainment p63
Shopping p65
400 m
0.25 miles
Royal Botanic Garden
Art Gallery of NSW
Art Gallery Rd
Shakespeare Pl
The Domain
Hospital Rd
Hyde Park Barracks Museum
Macquarie St
Museum of Sydney
Phillip La
Martin Place
Phillip St
Queens Square
St James' Church
St James Rd
St James
Prince Albert Rd
St Marys Rd
St Mary's Cathedral
College St
Cathedral St
St John Young Cres
Cook + Phillip Park
Archibald Memorial Fountain
Hyde Park
Elizabeth St
Macquarie Place
Bridge St
Young St
Bent St
Bligh St
O'Connell St
Abercrombie La
Spring St
Hunter St
Martin Pl
Dalley St
Bond St
Curtin Pl
Pitt St
Ash St
Angel Pl
Pitt St Mall
Sydney Tower Eye
Great Synagogue
Grosvenor St
Lang Park
Jamison St
Margaret St
Wynyard Park
Wynyard
Wynyard La
Carrington St
George St
York St
York La
Clarence St
King St
Kent St
Market St
Market Row
Druitt Pl
Druitt St
Western Distributor
Hickson Rd
Erskine St
Sussex St
Day St
Shelley St
Lime St
King Street Wharf
Pyrmont Bridge
Wheat Rd
Cockle Bay Wharf
Cockle Bay

Sights

Hyde Park Barracks Museum
MUSEUM

1 Map p52, D3

Convict architect Francis Greenway designed this squarish, decorously Georgian structure (1819) as convict quarters. Between 1819 and 1848, 50,000 men and boys did time here, most of whom had been sentenced by British courts to transportation to Australia for property crime. It later became an immigration depot, a women's asylum and a law court. These days it's a fascinating (if not entirely cheerful) museum, focusing on the barracks' history and the archaeological efforts that helped reveal it. (📞02-8239

2311; www.sydneylivingmuseums.com.au; Queens Sq, Macquarie St; adult/child $10/5; ◷10am-5pm; ⌷St James)

St Mary's Cathedral
CHURCH

2 Map p52, D4

Built to last, this 106m-long Gothic Revival–style cathedral was begun in 1868, consecrated in 1905 and substantially finished in 1928, but the massive, 75m-high spires weren't added until 2000. The crypt has an impressive terrazzo mosaic floor depicting the Creation, inspired by the Celtic-style illuminations of the *Book of Kells*. (📞02-9220 0400; www.stmaryscathedral.org.au; St Marys Rd; crypt $5; ◷6.30am-6.30pm; ⌷St James)

Understand
The Sydney Seige

On 15 December 2014, what Sydney had long feared appeared to be coming true when a lone gunman took 18 people hostage in the Lindt cafe in Martin Place. Shortly after, a black flag with an Islamic message was held against the window. After a 16-hour stand-off, shots were heard from inside and police stormed the cafe and killed the gunman. Two of the hostages were also killed – one by the gunman and one from the ricochet of a police bullet.

While the siege bore some of the hallmarks of a terrorist attack, it was soon revealed that the gunman was a lone, mentally disturbed person with a criminal record, unaligned with any terrorist group.

Sydney's Muslim community roundly condemned the attack and fears of a backlash were dissipated by messages of solidarity from leaders of other faiths and everyday Australians. The hashtag 'illridewithyou' quickly became a Twitter phenomenon, with tens of thousands of non-Muslim Australians offering their support to Muslims who felt nervous of retaliation.

KRZYSZTOF DYDYNSKI / GETTY IMAGES ©

Anzac Memorial and the Pool of Remembrance

Anzac Memorial
MEMORIAL

3 ⊙ Map p52, C5

Fronted by the Pool of Remembrance, this dignified art deco memorial (1934) commemorates the soldiers of the Australia and New Zealand Army Corps (Anzacs) who served in WWI. The interior dome is studded with 120,000 stars – one for each New South Welsh man and woman who served. These twinkle above Rayner Hoff's poignant sculpture *Sacrifice,* featuring a naked soldier draped over a shield and sword. There's also a small museum downstairs where a 13-minute film screens every 30 minutes. (www.anzacmemorial.nsw.gov.au; Hyde Park; admission free; ⊙9am-5pm; Museum)

Chinatown
AREA

4 ⊙ Map p52, B7

With a discordant soundtrack of blaring Canto pop, Dixon St is the heart and soul of Chinatown: a narrow, shady pedestrian mall with a string of restaurants and their urgently attendant spruikers. The ornate dragon gates *(paifang)* at either end are topped with fake bamboo tiles, golden Chinese calligraphy (with English translations), ornamental lions to keep evil spirits at bay and a fair amount of pigeon poo. (www.sydney-chinatown.info; Town Hall)

Sydney Tower Eye

TOWER

5 ⊙ Map p52, C3

The 309m-tall Sydney Tower (built 1970–81) offers unbeatable 360-degree views from the observation level 250m up – and even better ones for the daredevils braving the Skywalk on its roof. The visit starts with the 4D Experience – a short 3D film giving you a bird's-eye view (a parakeet's to be exact) of city, surf, harbour and what lies beneath the water, accompanied by mist sprays and bubbles; it's actually pretty darn cool. (☎1800 258 693; www.sydneytowereye.com.au; 100 Market St; adult/child $27/16, Skywalk adult/child $70/49; ⊙9am-9.30pm; ⊠St James)

Museum of Sydney

MUSEUM

6 ⊙ Map p52, D1

Built on the site of Sydney's first (and infamously pungent) Government House, the MoS is a fragmented, storytelling museum, which uses state-of-the-art installations to explore the city's people, places, cultures and evolution. The history of the Indigenous Eora people is highlighted – touching on the millennia of continuous occupation of this place. Be sure to open some of the many stainless-steel and glass drawers (they close themselves). (MoS; ☎02-9251 5988; www.sydneylivingmuseums.com.au; cnr Phillip & Bridge Sts; adult/child $10/5; ⊙9.30am-5pm; ⊠Circular Quay)

St James' Church

CHURCH

7 ⊙ Map p52, D3

Built from convict-made bricks, Sydney's oldest church (1819) is widely considered to be architect Francis Greenway's masterpiece. It was originally designed as a courthouse, but the brief changed and the cells became the crypt. Check out the dark-wood choir loft, the sparkling copper dome, the crypt and the 1950s stained-glass 'Creation Window'. (☎02-8227 1300; www.sjks.org.au; 173 King St; ⊙10am-4pm Mon-Fri, 9am-1pm Sat, 7am-4pm Sun; ⊠St James)

Great Synagogue

SYNAGOGUE

8 ⊙ Map p52, C4

The heritage-listed Great Synagogue (1878) is the spiritual home of Sydney's oldest Jewish congregation, established in 1831. It's considered the Mother Synagogue of Australia and is architecturally the most important in the southern hemisphere, combining Romanesque, Gothic, Moorish and Byzantine elements. Tours include the AM Rosenblum Museum's artefacts and a video presentation on Jewish beliefs, traditions and history in Australia. (☎02-9267 2477; www.great synagogue.org.au; 187a Elizabeth St; tours adult/child $10/5; ⊙tours noon Thu & 1st & 3rd Tue of the month; ⊠St James)

Sydney Town Hall HISTORIC BUILDING

9 ◉ Map p52, B5

Mansard roofs, sandstone turrets, wrought-iron trimmings and over-the-top balustrades: the French Second Empire wedding-cake exterior of the Town Hall (built 1868–89) is something to behold. Unless there's something on, you can explore the halls off the main entrance. The wood-lined concert hall has a humongous pipe organ with nearly 9000 pipes; it was once the largest in the world. It's used regularly for recitals, some of which are free. (www.sydneytownhall.com.au; 483 George St; ⏱8am-6pm Mon-Fri; 🚇Town Hall)

St Andrew's Cathedral CHURCH

10 ◉ Map p52, B5

Sporting beautiful stained glass and twin spires inspired by England's York Minster, squat St Andrew's Anglican church is the oldest cathedral in Australia (1868). Music is a big deal here; refer to the website for details of free lunchtime organ recitals, concert band performances and 'Young Music' concerts during school terms. The accomplished St Andy's choir warbles at various services. (☎02-9265 1661; www.sydneycathedral.com; cnr George & Bathurst Sts; ⏱10am-4pm Mon, Tue, Fri & Sat, 8am-7.30pm Wed & Sun, 10am-6.30pm Thu; 🚇Town Hall)

Eating

Tetsuya's FRENCH, JAPANESE $$$

11 Map p52, B5

Down a clandestine security driveway, this extraordinary restaurant is for those seeking a culinary journey rather than a simple stuffed belly. Settle in for 10-plus courses of French- and Japanese-inflected food from the creative genius of Japanese-born Tetsuya Wakuda. Book way ahead. (☎02-9267 2900; www.tetsuyas.com; 529 Kent St; degustation $220; ⏱noon-3pm Sat, 6-10pm Tue-Sat; 🚇Town Hall)

Rockpool MODERN AUSTRALIAN $$$

12 Map p52, C1

The Neil Perry empire now stretches to eight acclaimed restaurants in three cities, and this grand dining room is the mothership. After 25 years, Rockpool's creations still manage to wow diners. Expect crafty, contemporary cuisine with Asian influences, faultless service and an alluring wine list. (☎02-9252 1888; www.rockpool.com; 11 Bridge St; lunch mains $35-55, 9-/10-course dinner $145/165; ⏱noon-3pm Mon-Fri, 6-11pm Mon-Sat; 🚇Circular Quay)

Mr Wong CHINESE $$

13 Map p52, C1

Dumpling junkies shuffle down a dirty lane and into the bowels of an old warehouse for a taste of Mr Wong's

Local Life

Yum Cha

Despite the larger restaurants seating literally hundreds of dumpling devotees, there always seem to be queues in Chinatown on weekend mornings for yum cha. Literally meaning 'drink tea', it's really an opportunity to gorge on small plates of dim sum, wheeled between the tables on trolleys. Popular places include Din Tai Fung (p59) and, for vegetarians, **Bodhi** (☑02-9360 2523; www.bodhi.id.au; Cook + Phillip Park, 2-4 College St; dishes lunch $6.50-10, dinner $7-23; ⊙11am-4pm Mon, to 10pm Tue-Sun; ☑; ☒St James).

deliciously addictive Cantonese fare. There's a dark-edged glamour to the cavernous basement dining room. Despite seating 240, there are often queues out the door. (☑02-9240 3000; www.merivale.com.au/mrwong; 3 Bridge Lane; mains $25-38; ⊙noon-3pm & 5.30-11pm; ☒Wynyard)

Ippudo Sydney
JAPANESE $$

14 ☒ Map p52, C3

An exuberant chorus of welcome greets guests on arrival at this wonderful ramen house, tucked away near the Westfield food court. Founded in Fukuoka in 1985 and now in 11 countries, the Sydney branch serves all the soupy, noodley favourites. (☑02-8078 7020; www.ippudo.com.au; L5 Westfield Sydney, 188 Pitt St; mains $15-25; ⊙11am-10pm; ☒St James)

Mamak
MALAYSIAN $

15 ☒ Map p52, B6

Get here early (from 5.30pm) if you want to score a table without queuing, because this eat-and-run Malaysian joint is one of the most popular cheapies in the city. The satays are cooked over charcoal and are particularly delicious when accompanied by a flaky golden roti. (www.mamak.com.au; 15 Goulburn St; mains $6-17; ⊙11.30am-2.30pm & 5.30-10pm Mon-Thu, to 2am Fri & Sat; ☒Town Hall)

Est.
MODERN AUSTRALIAN $$$

16 ☒ Map p52, B1

Pressed-tin ceilings, huge columns, oversized windows and modern furniture make the interior design almost as interesting as the food. This is Sydney fine dining at its best; thick wallet and fancy threads a must. Seafood fills around half of the slots on the menu. (☑02-9240 3000; www.merivale.com.au/est; L1, 252 George St; 4-course lunch/dinner $118/155, degustation $180; ⊙noon-2.30pm Fri, 6-10pm Mon-Sat; ☒Wynyard)

Spice Temple
CHINESE $$

17 ☒ Map p52, C2

Tucked away in the basement of his Rockpool Bar & Grill is Neil Perry's darkly atmospheric temple to the cuisine of China's western provinces, especially Sichuan, Yunnan, Hunan, Jiangxi, Guangxi and Xingjiang. Expect plenty of heat and lots of thrills. (☑02-8078 1888; www.rockpool.com; 10

LARS RUECKER / GETTY IMAGES ©

Yum cha dishes

Bligh St; dishes $14-45; ⊘noon-3pm Mon-Fri, 6-10.30pm Mon-Sat; ✏; ☒Martin Place)

Din Tai Fung
CHINESE $$

18 ✖ Map p52, B6

The noodles and buns are great, but it's the dumplings that made this Taiwanese chain famous, delivering an explosion of fabulously flavoursome broth as you bite into their delicate casings. Come early, come hungry, come prepared to share your table. It also has stalls in The Star (p76) and Westfield Sydney (p65) food courts. (www.dintaifung.com.au; L1, World Sq, 644 George St; dishes $11-19; ⊘11.30am-2.30pm & 5.30-9pm; ☒Museum)

Alpha
GREEK $$

19 ✖ Map p52, C5

Located directly across from the Greek consulate in the grand dining room of the Hellenic Club, this wonderful restaurant brings all the zing and drama of the Mediterranean to the heart of the city. Chef Peter Conistis' menu covers the classics, with his own unique tweaks. (☎02-9098 1111; www.alpharestaurant.com.au; 238 Castlereagh St; mains $19-35; ⊘noon-3pm & 6-10pm; ☒Museum)

Central Baking Depot
BAKERY $

20 ✖ Map p52, A2

CBD produces quality baked goods right in the heart of the CBD (Central

Top Tip

Midnight Feasting

If jetlag or other lifestyle choices leave you with the midnight munchies, Haymarket is the best place in the city to be. Restaurants, even some of the very best ones, stay open late here (**Chat Thai** is open until 2am, for example), and on Chinatown's Dixon St you can find noodles to slurp at any time of night. Just don't expect service with a smile at 5am.

Business District). Drop by for a savoury snack (pies, sausage rolls, croissants, pizza slices, sandwiches), or a sweet treat with coffee. Seating is limited to a modest scattering of tables and a window bench. (www.central bakingdepot.com.au; 37-39 Erskine St; items $5-13; ⏲7am-4pm Mon-Sat; ⓇWynyard)

Drinking

Baxter Inn   BAR

21 Map p52, B3

Yes, it really is down that dark lane and through that unmarked door (it's easier to find if there's a queue; otherwise look for the bouncer lurking nearby). Whisky's the main poison and the friendly bar staff really know their stuff. (www.thebaxterinn.com; 152-156 Clarence St; ⏲4pm-1am Mon-Sat; ⓇTown Hall)

Frankie's Pizza   BAR

22 Map p52, C2

Descend the stairs and you'll think you're in a 1970s pizzeria, complete with plastic grapevines, snapshots covering the walls and tasty $6 pizza slices. But open the nondescript door in the corner and an indie wonderland reveals itself. Bands play here at least four nights a week (join them on Tuesdays for live karaoke) and there's another bar hidden below. (www.frankiespizzabytheslice.com; 50 Hunter St; ⏲4pm-3am Sun-Thu, noon-3am Fri & Sat; ⓇMartin Place)

Grandma's   COCKTAIL BAR

23 Map p52, B4

Billing itself as a 'retrosexual haven of cosmopolitan kitsch and faded granny glamour', Grandma's hits the mark. A stag's head greets you on the stairs and ushers you into a tiny subterranean world of parrot wallpaper and tiki cocktails. Someone's suprisingly cool granny must be very proud. (www.grandmasbarsydney.com; basement, 275 Clarence St; ⏲3pm-midnight Mon-Fri, 5pm-1am Sat; ⓇTown Hall)

Marble Bar   BAR

24 Map p52, B4

Built for a staggering £32,000 in 1893 as part of the Adams Hotel on Pitt St, this ornate underground bar is one of the best places in town for putting on the ritz (even if this is the Hilton).

Understand
Food Culture

Modern Australian

Those making the case for a distinctly Australian cuisine might point to 'bush tucker' or a degustation menu of pavlova, lamingtons, Vegemite sandwiches and Anzac biscuits. Patriots might suggest eating the coat of arms: kangaroo and emu, with a crocodile starter. A more reasoned approach has been taken by Australia's more innovative chefs, reverting to convict stereotypes: eyeing the surroundings, determining what to steal and weaving it all into something better than the sum of its parts – something perfect for the location and the climate.

This mix of European traditions with exotic flavours is casually termed Modern Australian cuisine – an amalgamation of Mediterranean, Asian, Middle Eastern and Californian cooking practices that emphasises lightness, experimentation and healthy eating. It's a hybrid style, shaped by migrant influences, climatic conditions and local ingredients – a culinary adventure built around local, seasonal produce that plays freely with imported ingredients and their accompanying cooking techniques and traditions. In Sydney this light-fingered culinary style has filtered down from sophisticated restaurants to modest main-street bistros and pubs.

The once ubiquitous phrase 'Mod Oz' may have fallen out of vogue, but the style of cooking is very much alive and well.

Current Trends

A craze for Latin American street food has seen tangy soft-shell tacos replace salt-and-pepper squid as the bar snack of choice in hipper establishments. A similar fad for 'dude food' has seen posh places adding fancy little burgers (called 'sliders' by those chefs who watch far too much American TV), pulled-pork sandwiches and big slabs of meat to their menus, often with a liberal side-serve of irony.

In an extension of the tapas trend that's been rolling for several years, 'shared plates' are all the rage. Bigger than tapas and not necessarily Spanish, this style of eating favours groups with adventurous palates. Fussy eaters and those from cultures that prefer their own portions on their own plates (we're looking at you, Brits) might find it more challenging.

Musos play anything from jazz to funk, Wednesday to Saturday. (www.marblebarsydney.com.au; basement, 488 George St; ☺4pm-midnight Sun-Thu, to 2am Fri & Sat; ඕTown Hall)

O Bar COCKTAIL BAR

25 Map p52, C1

At around $20, the cocktails at this 47th-floor revolving bar aren't cheap, but they're still cheaper than admission to Sydney Tower – and it's considerably more glamorous. The views are truly wonderful. (www.obardining.com.au; Level 47, Australia Sq, 264 George St; ☺5pm-late; ඕWynyard)

Rook COCKTAIL BAR

26 Map p52, B3

Seemingly designed for one-time grungsters turned stockbrokers, this covered rooftop bar has an artfully dishevelled look and serves a mean cocktail. It's not cheap though. Is spending $50 on lobster thermidor and then following it up with a deep-fried Mars Bar the ultimate ironic statement? (www.therook.com.au; L7, 56-58 York St; ☺noon-midnight Mon-Fri, 4pm to midnight Sat; ඕSt James)

Establishment BAR

Establishment's cashed-up crush proves that the art of swilling cocktails after a hard city day is not lost. Sit at the majestic marble bar or in the swish courtyard, or be absorbed by a leather lounge as stockbrokers scribble their phone numbers on the backs of coasters for flirty new acquaintances. Located at Est. (see 16 Map p52, B1) (www.merivale.com/establishmentbar; 252 George St; ☺11am-late Mon-Sat, noon-10pm Sun; ඕWynyard)

Good God Small Club BAR, CLUB

27 Map p52, B6

In a defunct underground taverna near Chinatown, Good God's rear dancetaria hosts everything from live indie bands to Jamaican reggae, '50s soul, rockabilly and tropical house music. Its success lies in the focus on great music rather than glamorous surrounds. (www.goodgodgoodgod.com; 55 Liverpool St; front bar free, club varies; ☺5-11pm Wed, to 1am Thu, to 3am Fri & Sat; ඕTown Hall)

Ivy BAR, CLUB

28 Map p52, B2

Hidden down a lane off George St, Ivy is a scarily fashionable complex of bars, restaurants, discreet lounges… even a swimming pool. It's also Sydney's most hyped venue; expect lengthy queues of suburban kids teetering on unfeasibly high heels, waiting to shed up to $40 on a Saturday for entry to Sydney's hottest club night, Pacha. (☎02-9254 8100; www.merivale.com/ivy; L1, 330 George St; ☺noon-late Mon-Fri, 6.30pm-late Sat; ඕWynyard)

Metro Theatre

Slip Inn & Chinese Laundry
PUB, CLUB

29 🚇 Map p52, A3

Slip in to this warren of moody rooms on the edge of Darling Harbour and bump hips with the kids. There are bars, pool tables, a beer garden and Mexican food, courtesy of El Loco. On Friday and Saturday nights the bass cranks up at the attached Chinese Laundry nightclub. (www.merivale.com.au/chineselaundry; 111 Sussex St; club $20-30; ⏱11am-late Mon-Fri, 4pm-late Sat; 🚇Wynyard)

Entertainment

Metro Theatre
LIVE MUSIC

30 ⭐ Map p52, B6

Easily Sydney's best venue for catching local and alternative international acts in intimate, well-ventilated, easy-seeing comfort. Other offerings include comedy, cabaret and dance parties. (📞02-9550 3666; www.metrotheatre.com.au; 624 George St; 🚇Town Hall)

State Theatre
THEATRE

31 Map p52, B4

The beautiful 2000-seat State Theatre is a lavish, gilt-ridden, chandelier-dangling palace. It hosts the Sydney Film Festival, concerts, comedy, opera, musicals and the odd celebrity chef. (☑02-9373 6655; www.statetheatre.com.au; 49 Market St; ☒St James)

Capitol Theatre
THEATRE

32 Map p52, B7

Lavishly restored, this large city theatre is home to long-running musicals (*Wicked, Les Misérables, Matilda*) and the occasional ballet or big-name concert. (☑1300 558 878; www.capitoltheatre.com.au; 13 Campbell St; ☒Central)

City Recital Hall
CLASSICAL MUSIC

33 Map p52, C2

Based on the classic configuration of the 19th-century European concert hall, this custom-built 1200-seat venue boasts near-perfect acoustics. Catch top-flight companies such as Musica Viva, the Australian Brandenburg Orchestra and the Australian Chamber Orchestra here. (☑02-8256 2222; www.cityrecitalhall.com; 2 Angel Pl; ☺box office 9am-5pm Mon-Fri; ☒Martin Place)

Musica Viva Australia
CLASSICAL MUSIC

Musica Viva is the largest presenter of ensemble music in the world, providing over 2000 concerts around Australia annually in a number of musical styles (including chamber music, a cappella, experimental and jazz). Sydney concerts are normally held at the City Recital Hall. (☑1800 688 482; www.mva.org.au)

Australian Brandenburg Orchestra
CLASSICAL MUSIC

The ABO is a distinguished part of Australia's artistic landscape, playing baroque and classical music on period-perfect instruments. Leading international guest artists appear frequently. Performances are usually held at the City Recital Hall. (☑02-9328 7581; www.brandenburg.com.au; tickets $71-166)

Pinchgut Opera
OPERA

This small player stages two intimate, oft-overlooked chamber operas every July and December at the City Recital Hall. (www.pinchgutopera.com.au)

Theatre Royal
THEATRE

34 Map p52, C3

Stages plays, musicals and revues; bookings through Ticketek. (www.theatreroyal.net.au; MLC Centre, 108 King St; ☒Martin Place)

Event Cinemas George St
CINEMA

35 Map p52, B5

An orgy of popcorn-fuelled mainstream entertainment, this monster movie palace has 18 screens and plenty of eateries and teen-centric distractions. All tickets are $13 on tight-arse Tuesday.

Queen Victoria Building

(☑02-9273 7300; www.eventcinemas.com.au; 505 George St; adult/child $20/15; ⏱sessions 9.30am-9.45pm; 🚇Town Hall)

Shopping

Queen Victoria Building

SHOPPING CENTRE

36 🔒 Map p52, B4

The magnificent QVB takes up a whole block and boasts nearly 200 shops on five levels. It's a High Victorian masterpiece – without doubt Sydney's most beautiful shopping centre. (QVB; www.qvb.com.au; 455 George St; ⏱11am-5pm Sun, 9am-6pm Mon-Wed, Fri & Sat, 9am-9pm Thu; 🚇Town Hall)

Strand Arcade

SHOPPING CENTRE

37 🔒 Map p52, B3

Constructed in 1891, the Strand rivals the QVB in the ornateness stakes. The three floors of designer fashions, Australiana and old-world coffee shops will make your shortcut through here considerably longer. (www.strandarcade. com.au; 412 George St; ⏱9am-5.30pm Mon-Wed & Fri, to 8pm Thu, 9am-4pm Sat, 11am-4pm Sun; 🚇St James)

Westfield Sydney

MALL

38 🔒 Map p52, C3

The city's most glamorous shopping mall is a bafflingly large complex gobbling up Sydney Tower and a fair chunk of Pitt Street Mall. The 5th-floor

Market City

food court is excellent. (www.westfield.com.au/sydney; 188 Pitt St Mall; ⊙9.30am-6.30pm Fri-Wed, to 9pm Thu; ⊠St James)

David Jones
DEPARTMENT STORE

39 🔒 Map p52, C3

DJs is Sydney's premier department store, occupying two enormous city buildings. The Castlereagh St store has women's and children's clothing; Market St has menswear, electrical goods and a high-brow food court. David Jones also takes up a sizeable chunk of **Westfield Bondi Junction** (☎02-9947 8000; www.westfield.com.au; 500 Oxford St; ⊙9.30am-6pm Fri-Wed, to 9pm Thu; ⊠Bondi Junction). (www.

davidjones.com.au; 86-108 Castlereagh St; ⊙9.30am-7pm Sat-Wed, to 9pm Thu & Fri; ⊠St James)

Myer
DEPARTMENT STORE

40 🔒 Map p52, B3

At seven storeys, Myer (formerly Grace Bros) is one of Sydney's largest stores and a prime venue for after-Christmas sales. It's marginally less swanky than David Jones, but you'll still find plenty of high-quality goods and some slick cafes. There's another branch at Westfield Bondi Junction. (☎02-9238 9111; www.myer.com.au; 436 George St; ⊙9am-7pm Fri-Wed, to 9pm Thu; ⊠St James)

Top Tip

City Shopping

The city centre's upmarket stores – centred on Pitt Street Mall, Market St and George St – offer plenty of choice for committed shopaholics. Shopping is also one of Chinatown's big drawcards, with countless bargains of the 'Made in China/Taiwan/Korea' variety. The insane buzz of Paddy's Markets is half the fun.

Kinokuniya
BOOKS

41 Map p52, B4

This outpost of the Japanese chain is the largest bookshop in Sydney, with over 300,000 titles. The comics section is a magnet for geeky teens – the imported Chinese, Japanese and European magazine section isn't. There's a cool little cafe here, too. (☎02-9262 7996; www.kinokuniya.com; L2, The Galeries, 500 George St; ⏰10am-7pm Fri-Wed, 10am-9pm Thu; ☒Town Hall)

Red Eye Records
MUSIC

42 Map p52, B4

Partners of music freaks beware: don't let them descend the stairs into this shop unless you are prepared for a lengthy delay. The shelves are stocked with an irresistible collection of new, classic, rare and collectable LPs, CDs, crass rock T-shirts, books, posters and music DVDs. (www.redeye.com.au; 143 York St; ⏰9am-6pm Fri-Wed, to 9pm Thu; ☒Town Hall)

RM Williams
CLOTHING, ACCESSORIES

43 Map p52, B3

Urban cowboys and country folk can't get enough of this hard-wearing outback gear. It's the kind of stuff politicians don when they want to seem 'fair dinkum' about something. Prime-ministerial favourites include Driza-Bone oilskin jackets, Akubra hats, moleskin jeans and leather work boots. There are also branches in Westfield Sydney (p65) and Westfield Bondi Junction. (www.rmwilliams.com.au; 389 George St; ⏰9am-6pm Fri-Wed, to 9pm Thu; ☒Wynyard)

Paddy's Markets
MARKET

44 Map p52, A7

Cavernous, 1000-stall Paddy's is the Sydney equivalent of Istanbul's Grand Bazaar, but swap the hookahs and carpets for mobile-phone covers, Eminem T-shirts and cheap sneakers. Pick up a VB singlet for Uncle Bruce or wander the aisles in capitalist awe. (www.paddysmarkets.com.au; 9-13 Hay St; ⏰10am-6pm Wed-Sun; ☒Central)

Market City
SHOPPING CENTRE

45 Map p52, B7

This large shopping centre above Paddy's Markets includes a big food court, heaps of discount fashion outlet shops (cheap Converse anyone?), a supermarket and video-game parlours. (www.marketcity.com.au; 9-13 Hay St; ⏰10am-7pm; ☒Central)

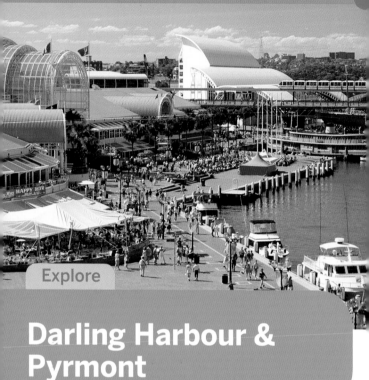

Explore

Darling Harbour & Pyrmont

Darling Harbour was once a thriving dockland, chock-full of factories, warehouses and shipyards. After decades of decline it was reinvented as a dedicated entertainment district, opening for the bicentennial in 1988. Dotted between the flyovers and fountains are some of the city's highest-profile attractions, while every other inch of the waterline is given over to bars and restaurants.

The Sights in a Day

☀ Start early with the morning tour of the **Sydney Fish Market** (p76) and then catch the light rail to the Exhibition stop. Take a peaceful stroll through the **Chinese Garden of Friendship** (p73) and then cross through **Tumbalong Park** (p75) to the western side of Darling Harbour. Spend the rest of the morning inspecting the ships, submarine and displays at the **Australian National Maritime Museum** (p73). For lunch, head to the Star's **Café Court** (p77) for dumplings at Din Tai Fung, followed by a sweet treat at **Adriano Zumbo** (p77).

☀ Across Pyrmont Bridge you'll find plenty to keep you (and the kids) amused for the rest of the afternoon. Three attractions are packed cheek-by-jowl; start with the **Sydney Sea Life Aquarium** (p70) and then – if you have the time, budget and inclination – tackle **Wild Life Sydney Zoo** (p75) and **Madame Tussauds** (p75).

☾ Have a sunset cocktail at **Flying Fish** (p77) then head on to **So-kyo** (p77) for accomplished Japanese food. Work off your meal with a stroll around the water's edge, watching the lights dancing on the water.

👁 **Top Sights**

Sydney Sea Life Aquarium (p70)

💗 **Best of Sydney**

Eating
Adriano Zumbo (p77)

Green Spaces
Chinese Garden of Friendship (p73)

Tumbalong Park (p75)

With Kids
Sydney Sea Life Aquarium (p70)

Monkey Baa Theatre Company (p79)

Getting There

🚃 **Train** Walk down to Darling Harbour from Wynyard or Town Hall stations.

🚊 **Light Rail** From Central or Glebe, the light rail is your best option. Stops include Exhibition, Pyrmont Bay, the Star and Fish Market.

⛴ **Ferry** Boats head from Circular Quay to Darling Harbour and Pyrmont Bay.

🚌 **Bus** Bus 443 heads from Circular Quay to the Maritime Museum.

Top Sights
Sydney Sea Life Aquarium

Even with its hefty admission charges, this large complex attracts stacks of visitors. Aside from standard wall-mounted tanks and ground-level enclosures, there are two large pools that you can walk through, safely enclosed in perspex tunnels, as an intimidating array of sharks and rays pass overhead. Residents of the penguin colony have lawless amounts of fun, while moon jellyfish billow through their disco-lit tube and an octopus keeps a wary eye on proceedings.

⊙ Map p72, D3

☏ 02-8251 7800

www.sydneyaquarium.com.au

Aquarium Pier

adult/child $40/28

🕑 9.30am-8pm

🚇 Town Hall

Sydney Sea Life Aquarium

Don't Miss

Sharks

Sharks get a bad rap, and one of the aquarium's biggest educational ambitions is to change perceptions of these misunderstood and endangered creatures. Mind you, coming up close to the impressive dentistry of the grey nurse sharks as they glide overhead will do little to allay fears.

Dugongs

The aquarium's two dugongs were rescued after washing up on different Queensland beaches. Attempts to return them to the wild failed, so the Dugong Island enclosure was built to house them. As sad as it is to see such large marine mammals in captivity, it offers a fascinating and rare opportunity to get close to them.

Japanese Spider Crabs

Forget the sharks, these giants from the deep are much creepier. The aquarium's specimens are mere tiddlers – they can grow to 4m claw to claw.

Great Barrier Reef

The colourful finale of the complex is this large tank (two million litres) filled with representatives of the multitude of creatures that inhabit Australia's most famous ecosystem. Sharks, sawfish, lobsters, clownfish, lionfish, angelfish, triggerfish, transsexual wrasses and swoon-worthy DayGlo corals all come together in the final floor-to-ceiling 'reef theatre'. Sit down and watch the show.

Talks & Feeds

Throughout the day there's a roster of scheduled talks in four different parts of the complex, with the highlights being the mid-morning ray, penguin and shark feeds (in separate enclosures, naturally!).

☑ Top Tips

▶ Sydney Sea Life Aquarium, Wild Life Sydney Zoo, Madame Tussauds, Sydney Tower Eye and Manly Sea Life Sanctuary are all run by the same company. You'll save a pretty penny on admission by purchasing combo tickets, which are available in almost every permutation of attractions.

▶ You'll save even more money by booking online.

▶ Arrive early to beat the crowds.

▶ Disabled access is good.

✗ Take a Break

On the edge of the King Street Wharf complex nearest to the Aquarium, Cargo Bar (p79) offers light snacks.

A similar distance in the opposite direction, **Pontoon** (Map p72, D4; ☎02-9267 7099; www.pontoonbar.com; The Promenade North, Cockle Bay Wharf; ◷11am-midnight Sun-Thu, to 4am Fri & Sat; ☒Town Hall) is a sometimes raucous bar that also serves casual meals.

A   B   C   D

*Sydney Harbour
(Port Jackson)*

Pyrmont Point
Park

Jones
Bay
Wharf ✕14

Darling
Point

Pirama Rd

Point St

Herbert St

Bowman St

13 🕭

1

Darling Island Rd

Community
Park

John St
Square

🕭

John St

Jones Bay Rd

*Pyrmont
Bay*

17 🕭

Erskine St

Western Distributor

Kent St

2

The Star

*Pyrmont
Bay Park*

King
Street
Wharf 7 🕭

Lime St

Shelley St

Sussex St

Pyrmont
Bay Wharf

*Pyrmont
Bay*

*Darling
Harbour*

18 🕭

King St

Day St

The
Star 8 ◉

Pyrmont
Rd

Harris St

Mount St

Pyrmont St

Edward St

12 ✕ 11 🕭
PYRMONT ✕
        10 ✕

Paternoster Rd

*Australian
National
Maritime
Museum*

Pyrmont
Bay

Union St

2 ◉

*Madame
Tussauds*

Wild Life 3 ◉ 4 ◉
Sydney Zoo ◉◉

**Sydney
Sea Life
Aquarium**

3

Miller St

Little Mount St

Harris St

Bulwara Rd

Jones St

Fish
Market 🕭

Bank St

Ada Pl

Experiment St

Harris St

Murray St

Bunn St

15 ✕

*Cockle
Bay*

Pyrmont Bridge

Harbourside

16 ✕

✕
Convention

*Cockle Bay
Wharf* 6 🕭

Wheat Rd

Day St

19 🕭

4

*Sydney Fish
Market* 9 🕭

Wattle Cres

Pyrmont Bridge Rd

Allen St

Darling Dr

Pyrmont St

20 ◎

5

Wentworth
Park

Wentworth
Park 🕭

Fig
Lane Park

Ada Pl

Wattle St Fig St

Western Distributor

**DARLING
HARBOUR**

ℹ Sydney
Visitor
Centre

★ 21

Tumbalong 5 ◎
Park

GLEBE

Exhibition
Centre ◎

*Chinese Garden
of Friendship* ◎ 1

Harbour St

0   200 m
0   0.1 miles

Ⓝ

Chinese Garden of Friendship

Sights

Chinese Garden of Friendship

GARDENS

1 ◉ Map p72, D5

Built according to Taoist principles, the Chinese Garden of Friendship is usually an oasis of tranquillity – although construction noise from Darling Harbour's redevelopment can intrude from time to time. Designed by architects from Guangzhou (Sydney's sister city) for Australia's bicentenary in 1988, the garden interweaves pavilions, waterfalls, lakes, paths and lush plant life. (☑02-9240 8888; www.chinesegarden.com.au; Harbour St; adult/child $6/3; ⊙9.30am-5pm; ☒Town Hall)

Australian National Maritime Museum

MUSEUM

2 ◉ Map p72, C3

Beneath an Utzon-like roof (a low-rent Opera House?), the Maritime Museum sails through Australia's inextricable relationship with the sea. Exhibitions range from Indigenous canoes to surf culture, to the navy. Entry includes free tours and there are kids' activities on Sundays. The 'big ticket' (adult/child $27/16) includes entry to the vessels moored outside, including the submarine HMAS *Onslow,* the destroyer HMAS *Vampire* and an 1874 square rigger, the *James Craig,* which periodically offers **sailing trips** (☑02-9298 3888; www.shf.org.au; Wharf 7, Pyrmont;

Understand

Beyond a Working Harbour

Building a Bustling Port

Sydney has always relied on its harbour. All sorts of cargo (including human, in the form of convicts) has been unloaded here, and some of the more interesting Sydney buildings are the utilitarian wharves and warehouses still lining parts of the harbour's inner shores. After the bubonic plague arrived in Sydney in 1900 (killing 103 Sydneysiders), the government took control of the old, privately owned wharves. Many ageing neoclassical warehouses were razed and replaced with new structures, some of them surprisingly elegant.

Decline & Revigoration

The 'containerisation' of shipping in the 1960s and '70s and the move of port activity to Botany Bay made many of the Edwardian wharves redundant almost overnight. Now, Sydneysiders' obsession with harbourside living is also putting many of these historic sites at risk. Fortunately, some have been transformed through inspired redevelopment – once-dilapidated sheds morphing into top-notch cafes, restaurants and apartments. Woolloomooloo's Finger Wharf, and the Walsh Bay and Pyrmont wharves, are classic examples.

Challenges

One of Sydney's big architectural challenges is to retain the rich heritage of a working harbour and to ensure these industrial sites have a successful role in the modern city. Critics condemn today's Darling Harbour as a tacky Las Vegan aberration, but few fail to be amazed at how completely this once-disused industrial space has been transformed.

In 2014 the wrecking balls got busy once again in Darling Harbour, this time attacking many of the major buildings erected in the 1980s in the first wave of redevelopment. The colossal convention and exhibition centres have gone and even bigger ones are scheduled to take their place (by late 2016). Further up the eastern shore, the Barangaroo complex is taking shape. This section of the harbour had continued to be used as a working wharf right up until 2006, when the final stevedoring operations were moved to Port Botany. It's now being transformed into an extension of the entertainment precinct, complete with hotels, apartments and Sydney's second major casino.

adult/child $150/50; 🚢Pyrmont Bay). Normally a replica of Cook's *Endeavour* also drops anchor. (📞02-9298 3777; www.anmm.gov.au; 2 Murray St; adult/child $7/3.50; 🕑9.30am-5pm; 🚊Pyrmont Bay)

Wild Life Sydney Zoo ZOO

 Map p72, D3

Complementing its sister and neighbour, Sea Life, this large complex houses an impressive collection of Australian native reptiles, butterflies, spiders, snakes and mammals (including kangaroos and koalas). The nocturnal section is particularly good, bringing out the extrovert in the quolls, potoroos, echidnas and possums. As interesting as Wild Life is, it's not a patch on Taronga Zoo. Still, it's worth considering as part of a combo with Sea Life, or if you're short on time. Tickets are cheaper online. (📞02-9333 9245; www.wildlifesydney.com.au; Aquarium Pier; adult/child $40/28; 🕑9.30am-7pm; 🚊Town Hall)

Madame Tussauds MUSEUM

4 Map p72, D3

In this celebrity-obsessed age, it's hardly surprising that Madame Tussauds' hyper-realistic waxwork dummies are just as popular now as when the eponymous madame lugged her macabre haul of French Revolution death masks to London in 1803. Where else do mere mortals get to strike a pose with Hugh Jackman and cosy up to Kylie? (www.madametussauds.com/sydney; Aquarium Pier; adult/child $40/28; 🕑9.30am-8pm; 🚊Town Hall)

Tumbalong Park PARK

5 Map p72, D5

Flanked by the new Darling Walk development, this grassy circle on Darling Harbour's southern rump is set up for family fun. Sunbakers and frisbee-throwers occupy the lawns; tourists dunk their feet in fountains on hot summer afternoons; and there's an excellent children's playground with a 21m flying fox. (🚊Town Hall)

Cockle Bay Wharf BUILDING

6 Map p72, D4

The first vaguely tasteful development in Darling Harbour, Cockle Bay Wharf occupies the harbour's cityside frontage as far as Pyrmont Bridge. Its sharp, contemporary angles are softened by the use of timber and whimsical sculptures (we particularly like the jaunty dancing storks). (www.cocklebaywharf.com; 🚊Town Hall)

King Street Wharf BUILDINGS

7 Map p72, D2

Cockle Bay Wharf in ultramodern metal drag, the $800-million King Street Wharf continues the Darling Harbour precinct north beyond Pyrmont Bridge. All the plush apartments are sold and the office space leased out, but you can still get a sniff of the high life at the waterfront bars and restaurants. (www.kingstreetwharf.com.au; Lime St; 🚊Wynyard)

Understand
Chinese in Australia

Chinese immigrants started to come to Australia in around 1840, when convict transportation ceased and labouring jobs became freely available. Initially they were considered a solution to labour shortages, but as gold-rush fever took hold, racial intolerance grew. The tireless Chinese were seen as threats, and state entry restrictions were enforced from the early 19th century into much of the 20th century.

In 1861 the NSW Government enacted the 'White Australia policy', aimed at reducing the influx of Chinese. This included a ban on naturalisation, work-permit restrictions and acts such as the 1861 Chinese Immigration Regulation & Restriction Act (an immigrant tax). The White Australia policy wasn't completely dismantled until 1973.

Today people of Chinese heritage make up 7.9% of Sydney's population, with well over half of these born in Australia.

The Star
CASINO

8 ◎ Map p72, B3

After a name change and a $961-million renovation, the Star reopened in late 2011 amid much hype and hoopla. The complex includes high-profile restaurants, bars, a nightclub, an excellent food court, a light rail station and the kind of high-end shops that will ensure that, in the unlikely event that you do happen to strike it big, a large proportion of your winnings will remain within the building. (☑02-9777 9000; www.star.com.au; 80 Pyrmont St; ⊙24hr; 🚇The Star)

Sydney Fish Market
MARKET

9 ◎ Map p72, A4

This piscatorial precinct on Blackwattle Bay shifts over 15 million kilograms of seafood annually, and has retail outlets, restaurants, a sushi bar, an oyster bar and a highly regarded cooking school. Chefs, locals and overfed seagulls haggle over mud crabs, Balmain bugs, lobsters and slabs of salmon at the daily fish auction, which kicks off at 5.30am weekdays. Check it out on a behind-the-scenes tour (adult/child $30/10). (☑02-9004 1108; www.sydneyfishmarket.com.au; Bank St; ⊙7am-4pm; 🚇Fish Market)

Darling Harbour Mini Train
TOUR

This people mover 'train' tootles around Darling Harbour (signal the driver to jump on board). It's good for the kids and for resting your legs. (☑0408 290 515; adult/child $5/4; ⊙10am-5pm)

Eating

Sokyo
JAPANESE $$$

10 ✕ Map p72, B3

Bringing an injection of Toyko glam to the edge of the casino complex, Sokyo serves well-crafted sushi and sashimi, delicate tempura, tasty robata grills and sophisticated mains. It also dishes up Sydney's best Japanese-style breakfast. Solo travellers should grab a counter seat by the sushi kitchen to watch all the action unfurl. (✆02-9657 9161; www.star.com.au/sokyo; The Star, 80 Pyrmont St; breakfast $23-38, set lunch $45, mains $30-58; ⏱7-10.30am & 5.30-11pm daily, noon-3pm Thu-Sat; 🚇The Star)

Adriano Zumbo
BAKERY $

11 ✕ Map p72, B3

The man who introduced Sydney to the macaron has indulged his Willy Wonka fantasies in this concept shop, where baked treats are artfully displayed amid pink neon. The macarons (or zumbarons, as they're known here), tarts, pastries and cakes are as astonishing to look at as they are to eat. (www.adrianozumbo.com; Café Court, The Star, 80 Pyrmont St; sweets $2.50-10; ⏱11am-9pm Sun, to 11pm Mon-Sat; 🚇The Star)

Café Court
FOOD COURT $

12 ✕ Map p72, B3

The Star has done a great job of filling its ground-floor food court with some of the best operators of their kind, such as Din Tai Fung (p59) for dump-lings, Messina (p110) for gelato and Adriano Zumbo for sweet delights. (www.star.com.au; ground fl, The Star; mains $10-18; ⏱11am-9pm Sun & Mon, to 11pm Tue-Sat; 🚇The Star)

Cafe Morso
CAFE $$

13 ✕ Map p72, B1

The most popular eatery along Jones Bay Wharf, Morso lures black-clad, laptop-focused business bods and yacht skippers. Sassy breakfasts morph into proper cooked lunches, or you can just grab a sandwich (around $8). (✆02-9692 0111; www.cafemorso.com. au; Jones Bay Wharf; breakfast $16-19, lunch $17-27; ⏱7am-4pm; 🚇The Star)

Flying Fish
SEAFOOD $$$

14 ✕ Map p72, B1

Beyond the architects and investment groups along Jones Bay Wharf is this romantic seafood restaurant. The city lights work their magic all too easily here, aided by excellent food and an indulgent cocktail list. Aside from all that romance stuff, it has the coolest toilets in town – the clear-glass stalls frost over when you close the door. (✆02-9518 6677; www.flyingfish.com.au; Jones Bay Wharf; mains $47-49; ⏱noon-2.30pm daily, 6-10.30pm Mon-Sat; 🚇The Star)

Kazbah
NORTH AFRICAN $$

15 ✕ Map p72, C4

Rock the Kazbah for beautifully presented, tasty dishes from the Maghreb and Middle East, including exceptional

> ## Understand
> ### The Rum Rebellion
> -
>
> When Governor Phillip returned to England in 1792, Francis Grose took over. Grose granted land to officers of the New South Wales Corps, nicknamed the Rum Corps. With so much money, land and cheap labour in their hands, this military leadership made huge profits at the expense of small farmers. They began paying for labour and local products in rum. Meeting little resistance (everyone was drunk), they managed to upset, defy, outmanoeuvre and out-last three governors, the last of which was William Bligh, the famed captain of the mutinous ship *HMAV Bounty*. In 1808 the Rum Corps ousted Bligh from power in what became known as the Rum Rebellion.
>
> The Rum Rebellion was the final straw for the British government – in 1809 it decided to punish its unruly child. Lieutenant Colonel Lachlan Macquarie was dispatched with his own regiment and ordered the New South Wales Corps to return to London to get their knuckles rapped. Having broken the stranglehold of the Rum Corps, Governor Macquarie began laying the groundwork for social reforms.

tagines. There's a good value 'express lunch' menu for those short on time or cash. The original restaurant in Balmain (p43) is that suburb's best eatery. (02-9555 7067; www.kazbah.com.au; The Promenade, Harbourside; lunch $10-29, dinner $28-35; 11.30am-3pm & 5.30-9.30pm; Convention)

Zaaffran   INDIAN $$

16 Map p72, C4

In a city with a gazillion cheap Indian joints, Zaaffran is a stand-out. Authentic and innovative curries by chef Vikrant Kapoor are served up with awesome views across Darling Harbour's sparkle and sheen. Book a terrace seat and launch yourself into the tiger prawn coconut curry. There's a good vegetarian selection, too.

(02-9211 8900; www.zaaffran.com.au; L2, Harbourside; mains $20-35; noon-2.30pm & 6-10.15pm; ; Convention)

Drinking

Loft   BAR

17 Map p72, D2

The Loft is far from lofty – it's more like an open-plan office space – but the walls fold back and disappear, sweeping your eye out across Darling Harbour and beyond. Interior design is Moroccan chic and service is snappy. Book for high tea at high noon on Saturday and Sunday. Live music on Fridays. (02-9299 4770; www.theloftsydney.com; 3 Lime St, King St Wharf;

🕒 4pm-1am Mon-Thu, noon-3am Fri & Sat, noon-1am Sun; 🚇 Wynyard)

Cargo Bar
BAR

 18 Map p72, D3

This pioneering King Street Wharf bar still lures beautiful boys, babes and backpackers, who get wall-to-wall boozy after 11pm. Before the drinkers descend, savour the harbour views, tasty pizzas and salads. DJs fire things up on the weekend. (📞02-9262 1777; www.cargobar.com.au; 52 The Promenade, King St Wharf; 🕒11am-midnight Sun-Thu, to 3am Fri & Sat; 🚇Wynyard)

Home
CLUB, BAR

 19 Map p72, D4

Welcome to the pleasuredome: a three-level, 2100-capacity timber and glass 'prow' that's home to a dance floor, countless bars, outdoor balconies, and sonics that make other clubs sound like transistor radios. You can catch live music most nights at the attached Tokio Hotel bar downstairs (www.tokiohotellive.com.au), but the club itself is reserved for special events, often featuring big-name DJs. (www.homesydney.com; 1 Wheat Rd, Cockle Bay Wharf; 🚇Town Hall)

Entertainment

IMAX
CINEMA

 20 Map p72, D4

It's big bucks for a 45-minute movie, but everything about IMAX is big, and this is reputedly the biggest IMAX in the world. The eight-storey screen shimmers with kid-friendly documentaries (sharks, interstellar etc) as well as blockbuster features, many in 3D. (📞02-9281 3300; www.imax.com.au; 31 Wheat Rd; adult/child short $23/17, feature $34/24; 🕒sessions 10am-10pm; 🚇Town Hall)

Monkey Baa Theatre Company
THEATRE

 21 Map p72, D5

If you can drag them away from the neighbouring playground, bring your budding culture vultures here to watch Australian children's books come to life. This energetic company devises and stages their own adaptations. (📞02-8624 9340; www.monkeybaa.com.au; 1 Harbour St; tickets $25; 🚇Town Hall)

Sydney Lyric
THEATRE

This 2000-seat theatre within the Star (see 8 ⊙ Map p72, B3) casino stages big-name musicals and the occasional concert. (📞02-9509 3600; www.sydneylyric.com.au; The Star, Pirrama Rd; 🚇The Star)

Explore

Inner West

The Inner West is a sociological stew of students, goths, urban hippies, artists, Indigenous Australians, Mediterranean immigrants and sexual subculturalists. Newtown shadows King St, lined with interesting boutiques, bookshops, yoga studios, cafes and an inordinate number of Thai restaurants. It's definitely climbing the social rungs, but Newtown is still free-thinking and bolshy. Glebe is similar, if a little quieter.

The Sights in a Day

Begin your day at the **Power-house Museum** (p86), where there's more than enough to keep you occupied for most of the morning. Catch the light rail to the Jubilee stop and pay a quick visit to **Sze Yup Temple** (p87) before walking around **Jubilee & Bicentennial Parks** (p88) to Blackwattle Bay. If you feel like indulging, stop at the **Boathouse on Blackwattle Bay** (p89) for lunch.

Catch a cab to the **White Rabbit** (p86) gallery, then hop up to Newtown where you can spend the remainder of the afternoon shopping on King St. Take a short detour down Church St to explore the cobwebby corners of **Camperdown Cemetery** (p86).

Grab dinner on King St. If you're not booked for a show at **Carriageworks** (p86), hit the local bars. A short pub-crawl route could include **Corridor** (p91), **Zanzibar** (p92), the **Courthouse Hotel** (p92), **Midnight Special** (p91) and **Earl's Juke Joint** (p90). Or continue on to **Newtown Social Club** (p93) to catch a band, or to the **Imperial Hotel** (p92) for the Priscilla drag show.

For a local's day in the Inner West, see p82.

 Local Life

Studying the University of Sydney (p82)

 Best of Sydney

Bars & Pubs
Courthouse Hotel (p92)

With Kids
Powerhouse Museum (p86)

Gay & Lesbian
Imperial Hotel (p92)

Birdcage at Zanzibar (p92)

For Free
White Rabbit (p86)

Nicholson Museum (p83)

Getting There

Train Newtown is particularly well served by trains, with four stations (Macdonaldtown, Newtown, Erskineville and St Peters) on three train lines (Inner West, South and Bankstown).

Light Rail Glebe has two MLR stops in its back streets (Glebe and Jubilee Park).

Bus Dozens of buses from the city ply Glebe Point Rd, Parramatta Rd and City Rd/King St.

Local Life
Studying the University of Sydney

Australia's oldest tertiary institution (1850) has more than 45,000 students and even boasts its own postcode. You don't need to have a PhD to grab a free campus map and wander around. The university completely dominates the surrounding suburbs of Camperdown, Darlington, Chippendale, and to a lesser extent, Glebe and Newtown.

❶ Scope out the Seymour Centre

Behind a glass curtain wall on an insanely busy intersection, the Sydney Uni–affiliated **Seymour Centre** (☎02-9351 7940; www.seymourcentre.com; cnr City Rd & Cleveland St; ☒Redfern) shows an eclectic selection of plays, cabaret, comedy and musicals in its four theatres. Drop by to see what's on during your stay.

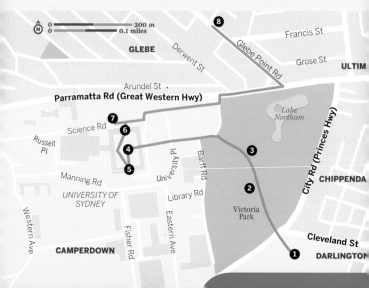

❷ Venture into Victoria Park

The green gateway to the Inner West and the University of Sydney, **Victoria Park** (cnr Parramatta & City Rds; 🚇Redfern) is a 9-hectare grassy wedge revolving around pond-like Lake Northam. In February, 75,000 people descend on the park for the Mardi Gras Fair Day: dog shows, live performances and the 'Miss Fair Day' drag competition.

❸ Dip into Victoria Park Pool

This 50m heated outdoor **pool** (📞02-9518 4800; www.vppool.com.au; cnr Parramatta & City Rds; adult/child $6/4.50; ⏰6am-7pm; 🚌431-440) in Victoria Park serves as Newtown and Glebe's beach. It also has a gym ($18 with pool access), crèche, cafe and swim shop.

❹ Cross the Quadrangle

Flanked by two grand halls that wouldn't be out of place in Harry Potter's beloved Hogwarts, the Quadrangle has a Gothic Revival design that tips its mortarboard towards the stately colleges of Oxford. It was designed by colonial architect Edward Blacket and completed in 1862; he also built St Andrew's Cathedral in the city.

❺ Nick into the Nicholson

The **Nicholson Museum** (www.sydney.edu.au/museums; University Pl; admission free; ⏰10am-4.30pm Mon-Fri, noon-4pm 1st Sat of month; 🚌422-440) is a must-see for ancient history geeks, with its amazing accumulation of Greek, Roman, Cypriot, Egyptian and Near Eastern antiquities. It was founded

in 1860 by orphan-made-good Sir Charles Nicholson, a key figure in the establishment of the university.

❻ Peruse the University Art Gallery

Founded at the same time as the university, this **gallery** (www.sydney.edu.au/museums; Science Rd; admission free; ⏰10am-4.30pm Mon-Fri, noon-4pm 1st Sat of month; 🚌422-440) has accumulated over 7000 works of Aboriginal, Australian, East Asian and European art. Alongside the likes of Goya and Chagall are other important Australian artists: Sidney Nolan, Arthur Boyd, Grace Cossington Smith...

❼ Meander through the Macleay

Nearby, the **Macleay Museum** (www.sydney.edu.au/museums; Science Rd; admission free; ⏰10am-4.30pm Mon-Fri, noon-4pm 1st Sat of month; 🚌422-440) is the oldest natural-history museum in Australia, having its roots in the collection of the Macleay family (of Elizabeth Bay House fame). It also has a historic photographic collection and an early assemblage of Aboriginal, Torres Strait and Pacific Island material.

❽ Slink into Sappho Books

Combining the essentials of student life – books, coffee, alcohol and lesbian poetry – Sappho's has a beaut bohemian garden **cafe** (📞02-9552 4498; www.sapphobooks.com.au; 51 Glebe Point Rd; tapas $5-12, mains $8-19; ⏰9am-7pm Sun, 7.30am-7pm Mon & Tue, to 10pm Wed-Sat; 🍴; 🚌Glebe), its walls scrawled with generations of graffiti. Wine and tapas kick in after 6pm.

For reviews see

◎	Sights	p86
⊗	Eating	p88
⊗	Drinking	p90
⊗	Entertainment	p93
⊗	Shopping	p95

500 m
0.25 miles

REDFERN

Balfe St

Cleveland St

Edward St

Ivy St

Lawson St

Gibbons St

Regent St

Cope St

Botany Rd

Wyndham St

Henderson Rd

Garden St

Gerard St

Phillips St

DARLINGTON

Lander St

Abercrombie St

Wilson St

Rose St

Darlington Rd

EVELEIGH

⊗3
Carriageworks

Lyne St

Sutor St

Copeland St

Dibbs St

Newton St

Mitchell Rd

Belmont St

ERSKINEVILLE

Ashmore St

CITY RD (PRINCES HWY)

UNIVERSITY OF SYDNEY

Fisher Rd

Western Ave

Carillon Ave

Campbell St

Forbes La

Wilson St

⊗ 36
29

Hollis Park

Jack Park
Haynes Reserve

Railway Pde

Park St

Swanson St

Binning St

Malcolm St

Erskineville

⊗ Macdonaldtown

Burren St

Bridge St

Charles St

George St

Prospect St

Amy St

24 27

Royal Prince Alfred Hospital

Missenden Rd

CAMPERDOWN

13 ⊗

25 ⊗
21 ⊗

Hordern St

Egan St

Watkin St

Watkin La

John St

Green Bans Park

Union St

Gowrie St

⊗ 23

Church St

38

31

Northwood St

Roberts St

Hopetoun St

Australia St

4 ⊗

12 35

26

22

17

41 ⊗

Newtown

Newman St

Norfolk St

⊗ 14

39 ⊗

NEWTOWN

9 ⊗

King St (Princes Hwy)

⊗ 32

Camden St

Alice St

Kent St

Fulham St

Sloane St

Pemell St

Enmore Rd

Linthorpe St

19

28

18

37

30

15 ⊗

Gladstone St

Probert St

Chelmsford St

Oxford St

Baltic St

Denison St

Camperdown Cemetery

Salisbury Rd

Mallett St

Fowler St

Ross St

Australia St

Church St

Dunblane St

Sights

White Rabbit

GALLERY

1 Map p84, E4

If you're an art lover or a bit of a Mad Hatter, this particular rabbit hole will leave you grinning like a Cheshire Cat. There are so many works in this private collection of cutting-edge, contemporary Chinese art, that only a fraction can be displayed at one time. Who knew that the People's Republic was turning out work that was so edgy, funny, sexy and idiosyncratic? (www.whiterabbitcollection.org; 30 Balfour St; admission free; ☉10am-5pm Wed-Sun, closed Feb & Aug; ☒Redfern)

Powerhouse Museum

MUSEUM

2 Map p84, E3

A short walk from Darling Harbour, this science and design museum whirs away inside the former power station for Sydney's defunct, original tram network. High-voltage interactive demonstrations wow school groups with the low-down on how lightning strikes, magnets grab and engines growl. It's a huge hit with kids but equally popular with adults, touching on subjects such as fashion and furniture design. (☑02-9217 0111; www.powerhousemuseum.com; 500 Harris St; adult/child $15/8; ☉9.30am-5pm; ☒Paddy's Markets)

Local Life

Chippendale

Tucked between Central station, Surry Hills and Sydney University, the tiny suburb of Chippendale is one to watch. The 2009 opening of the White Rabbit gallery was an early herald of what is steadily turning into one of Sydney's coolest neighbourhoods. Now, as the Jean Nouvel/Sir Norman Foster–driven Central Park complex of sustainable plant-covered towers and terraces is taking shape, fantastic new eateries and bars are already springing up. Watch this space.

Carriageworks

ARTS CENTRE

3 Map p84, D6

Built between 1880 and 1889, this intriguing group of huge Victorian-era workshops was part of the Eveleigh Railyards. The rail workers chugged out in 1988 and in 2007 the artists pranced in. It's now home to various avant-garde arts and performance projects, and there's usually something interesting to check out. (www.carriageworks.com.au; 245 Wilson St; admission free; ☉10am-6pm; ☒Redfern)

Camperdown Cemetery

CEMETERY

4 Map p84, B6

Take a self-guided tour beyond the monstrous 1848 fig tree into this dark,

OLIVER STREWE / GETTY IMAGES ©

Sze Yup Temple

eerily unkempt cemetery next to St Stephens Church. Famous Australians buried here between 1849 and 1942 include Eliza Donnithorne, the inspiration for Miss Havisham in Dickens' *Great Expectations* (📞02-9557 2043; www.neac.com.au; 189 Church St; tours $10; ☀sunrise-sunset, tours 11.30am 1st Sun of the month Feb-Dec; 🚃Newtown)

Central Park
AREA

5 ◎ Map p84, E4

Occupying the site of an old brewery, this work-in-progress residential and shopping development will eventually cover 6500 sq metres, and is already revitalising the central fringe suburb of Chippendale. Most impressive is

Jean Nouvel's award-winning, vertical garden–covered tower, **One Central Park** (2013; 117m). The cantilevered roof has been designed to reflect sunlight onto the greenery below. A striking new Frank Gehry building is being built on the University of Technology campus across Broadway. (www.centralparksydney.com; Broadway; 🚃Central Station)

Sze Yup Temple
TEMPLE

6 ◎ Map p84, B2

This humble backstreet temple was opened in 1898 by immigrants from the Sze Yup area of China. It's dedicated to 3rd-century folk hero Kwan Ti, whose embroidered, green-robed image, flanked by two guards, takes centre stage on the altar. Known for his loyalty, physical prowess and masculinity, he is looked to by supplicants as a wise judge, guide and protector. (☏02-9660 6465; 2 Edward St; ⏱10am-5pm; 🚊Jubilee Park)

Jubilee & Bicentennial Parks

PARK

7 Map p84, A2

These two rolling, grassy parks merge together to offer some tasty views across Rozelle Bay, and of both the Anzac and Harbour Bridges. Massive fig and palm trees dot the lawns. A path leads from here along the shoreline to Blackwattle Bay, passing the Victorian Italianate **Bellevue Cottage** (1896) and a park built around the templelike ruins of an industrial incinerator. (Glebe Point Rd; 🚊Jubilee Park)

Eating

Ester

MODERN AUSTRALIAN $$

8 Map p84, E5

Ester breaks the trend for hip new eateries by accepting bookings, but in other respects it exemplifies Sydney's contemporary dining scene: informal but not sloppy; innovative without being overly gimmicky; hip, but never try-hard. Influences straddle continents and dishes are made to be shared. If humanly possible, make room for dessert. (☏02-8068 8279; www.ester-restaurant.com.au; 46 Meagher St; mains $26-36; ⏱noon-5pm Sun, noon-3pm Fri, 6pm-late Tue-Sat; 🚊Redfern)

Eveleigh Farmers' Market

MARKET $

Over 70 regular stallholders sell their goodies at Sydney's best farmers market, held in a heritage-listed railway workshop at Carriageworks (see 3 ⊙ Map p84, D6). Food and coffee stands do a brisk business; celebrity chef Kylie Kwong can often be spotted cooking up a storm. (www.eveleighmarket.com.au; Carriageworks, 245 Wilson St; ⏱8am-1pm Sat; 🚊Redfern)

Black Star Pastry

BAKERY $

9 Map p84, B7

Wise folks follow the Black Star to pay homage to excellent coffee, a large selection of sweet things and a few very good savoury things (gourmet pies and the like). There are only a couple of tables; it's more a snack-and-run or

picnic-in-the-park kind of place. (www.
blackstarpastry.com.au; 277 Australia St;
mains $7-10; ⏱7am-5pm; 🚊Newtown)

Glebe Point Diner
MODERN AUSTRALIAN $$$

10 🍴 Map p84, B2

A sensational neighbourhood diner,
where only the best local produce
is used and everything – from the
home-baked bread and hand-churned
butter to the nougat finale – is made
from scratch. The food is creative and
comforting at the same time; a rare
combination. (☎02-9660 2646; www.
glebepointdiner.com.au; 407 Glebe Point Rd;
mains $29-39; ⏱noon-3pm Thu-Sun, 6-11pm
Mon-Sat; 🚊Jubilee Park)

Boathouse on Blackwattle Bay
SEAFOOD $$$

11 🍴 Map p84, C1

The best restaurant in Glebe, and one of
the best seafood restaurants in Sydney.
Offerings range from oysters so fresh
you'd think you shucked them yourself,
to a snapper pie that'll go straight to the
top of your favourite-dish list. Amazing
Anzac Bridge views; reservations essential. (☎02-9518 9011; www.boathouse.net.
au; 123 Ferry Rd; mains $41-48; ⏱noon-3pm
Fri-Sun, 6-11pm Tue-Sun; 🚊Glebe)

Mary's
BURGERS $

12 🍴 Map p84, B7

Not put off by the grungy aesthetics,
the ear-splitting heavy metal or the
fact that the building was previously a
sexual health clinic and a Masonic Temple? Then head up to the mezzanine of
this dimly lit hipster bar for some of
the best burgers and fried chicken in
town. (6 Mary St; mains $14; ⏱4pm-midnight
Mon-Sat, noon-10pm Sun; 🚊Newtown)

Luxe
CAFE $$

13 🍴 Map p84, B6

Campos (p90), next door, might be the
pinnacle of Sydney's caffeine culture,
but if you want to sit down, read
the paper and eat something more
substantial, Luxe is the dux. The menu
stretches to cooked brekkies, pasta
and burgers, and the counter of this
industrial-chic bakery-cafe is chocka
with chunky sandwiches, moist cakes
and delicate tarts. (www.luxesydney.com.
au; 191 Missenden Rd; breakfast $8-20, lunch
$11-22; ⏱8am-4pm; 🚊Macdonaldtown)

Bloodwood
MODERN AUSTRALIAN $$

14 🍴 Map p84, B7

Relax over a few drinks and a progres-
sion of small plates (we love those
polenta chips!) in the front bar, or
make your way to the rear to enjoy
soundly conceived and expertly cooked
dishes from across the globe. The decor
is industrial-chic and the vibe is alternative – very Newtown. (☎02-9557 7699;
www.bloodwoodnewtown.com; 416 King St;
dishes $9-30; ⏱5-11pm Mon-Fri, noon-11pm
Sat & Sun; 🚊Newtown)

Local Life

Killer Cafes

The Inner West is one of Sydney's most well caffeinated neighbourhoods. King of the bean scene is cramped **Campos** (02-9516 3361; www.camposcoffee.com; 193 Missenden Rd; pastries $4; 7am-4pm; Macdonaldtown), where food is limited to tasty pastries. There's rather more solid sustenance on offer at **Fleetwood Macchiato** (43 Erskineville Rd; mains $9-18; 7am-3pm; ; Erskineville) – delicious cooked breakfasts, tasty sandwiches and homemade everything – plus it's got the best name of any cafe ever. **Vargabar Espresso** (02-9517 1932; www.vargabarnewtown.com.au; 10 Wilson St; mains $10-16; 7am-6pm; ; Newtown) is a diminutive dark-pink cafe with an electric-blue coffee machine, known for its brews and substantial breakfasts.

Cow & the Moon
ICE CREAM $

15 Map p84, A7

Forget the diet and slink into this cool corner cafe, where an array of sinful truffles and tasty tarts beckons seductively. Ignore them and head straight for the world's best gelato – the title this humble little place won in 2014 at the Gelato World Tour in Rimini, Italy. (181 Enmore Rd; small gelati $5; 9am-11pm; Newtown)

Yuga
CAFE $$

16 Map p84, C4

What a sweet-smelling combo: a florist *and* a cafe that's stylish, reasonably priced and friendly. The menu at sophisticated and serene Yuga starts with Aussie breakfasts and morphs into Italian lunches. (02-9692 8604; www.yugaflora.com.au; 172 St Johns Rd; breakfast $12-16, lunch $12-20; 7am-4pm; Glebe)

Thai Pothong
THAI $$

17 Map p84, B7

The menu at this crowd-pleasing restaurant is predictable and the usual crowd of golden Buddhas festoons the walls, but the mood is oddly romantic. Pull up a window seat and watch the Newtowners pass by. (02-9550 6277; www.thaipothong.com.au; 294 King St; mains $15-31; noon-3pm & 6-10.30pm; ; Newtown)

Drinking

Earl's Juke Joint
BAR

18 Map p84, B7

The current it-bar of the minute, swinging Earl's serves craft beers and killer cocktails to the Newtown hiperati. (407 King St; 4pm-midnight Mon-Sat, to 10pm Sun; Newtown)

MICHAEL TAYLOR / GETTY IMAGES ©

Thai Pothong

Midnight Special

BAR

19 Map p84, A7

Band posters and paper lanterns decorate the black walls of this groovy little bar. Musicians take to the tiny stage a couple of nights a week. (www.themidnightspecial.com.au; 44 Enmore Rd; ☺5pm-midnight Tue-Sat, to 10pm Sun; ☒Newtown)

Friend in Hand Hotel

PUB

20 Map p84, D3

At heart Friend in Hand is still a working-class pub with a resident loud-mouth cockatoo and a cast of grizzly old-timers and local larrikins propping up the bar. But then there's all the other stuff: live music, life drawing, poetry readings, crab racing, comedy nights. Strewth Beryl, bet you weren't expecting that. (☎02-9660 2326; www.friendinhand.com.au; 58 Cowper St; ☺10am-10pm Sun, 8am-midnight Mon-Sat; ☎; ☒Glebe)

Corridor

COCKTAIL BAR

21 Map p84, B6

The name exaggerates this bar's skinniness, but not by much. Downstairs the bartenders serve old-fashioned cocktails and a good range of wine, while upstairs there's interesting art (for sale) and a tiny deck. There's live music most nights. (www.corridorbar.com.au; 153a King St; ☺5pm-midnight Mon, 3pm-midnight Tue-Sun; ☒Newtown)

Zanzibar

BAR

22 ⊜ Map p84, B7

Eastern opulence continues all the way to the roof at this late-night Newtown bar with a winged art deco facade. Catch the sunset from the rooftop, settle into a cushioned couch or shoot pool in the funky downstairs bar. On Wednesday nights the Birdcage lesbian night takes over the 2nd floor. (☑02-9519 1511; www.zanzibar newtown.com.au; 323 King St; ⊘10am-4am Mon-Sat, 11am-midnight Sun; ⊠Newtown)

Imperial Hotel

GAY, CLUB

23 ⊜ Map p84, B7

The art deco Imperial is legendary as the setting for *The Adventures of Priscilla, Queen of the Desert*. The front bar is a lively place for pool-shooting and cruising, with the action shifting to the cellar club late on a Saturday night. But it's in the cabaret bar that the legacy of Priscilla is kept alive. (www.theimperialhotel.com.au; 35 Erskineville Rd; admission free-$15; ⊘3pm-midnight Sun-Thu, to 5am Fri & Sat; ⊠Erskineville)

Hive

BAR

24 ⊜ Map p84, C7

In increasingly groovy Erskineville village, this breezy little corner bar lures the neighbourhood's hipsters with food, cocktails, DJs spinning funk and soul, crazy murals and a quiet bolt-hole upstairs. Order a few plates to share over a glass of vino and pull up a footpath table. (☑02-9519 9911; www.thehivebar.com.au; 93 Erskineville Rd;

⊘noon-midnight Mon-Sat, 11am-10pm Sun; ⊠Erskineville)

Marlborough Hotel

PUB, CLUB

25 ⊜ Map p84, B6

One of many great old art deco pubs in Newtown, the Marly has a front sports bar with live bands on weekends and a shady beer garden. Head upstairs for soul food and rockabilly bands at Miss Peaches, or downstairs for all sorts of kooky happenings at the Tokyo Sing Song nightclub. (☑02-9519 1222; www.marlboroughhotel. com.au; 145 King St; ⊘10am-4am Mon-Sat, noon-midnight Sun; ⊠Macdonaldtown)

Courthouse Hotel

PUB

26 ⊜ Map p84, B7

What a brilliant pub! A block back from the King St fray, the 150-year-old Courthouse is the kind of place where everyone from pool-playing goth lesbians to magistrates can have a beer and feel right at home. How ironic – a complete absence of social judgement in a pub called the Courthouse. Good pub grub, too. (202 Australia St; ⊘10am-midnight Mon-Sat, to 10pm Sun; ⊠Newtown)

Rose of Australia

PUB

27 ⊜ Map p84, C7

The extensive renovations to this old corner pub haven't dented the tiled front bar's charm. Locals of all persuasions hang out here, catching some afternoon rays at the streetside tables, a footy game on the big screens or a meal upstairs. (☑02-9565

> ## Understand
> **An Australian Identity**
>
> The Commonwealth of Australia came into being on 1 January 1901 and New South Wales became a state of the new Australian nation. Yet Australia's legal ties with, loyalty to and dependency on Britain remained strong. When WWI broke out in Europe, Australian troops were sent to fight in the trenches of France, at Gallipoli in Turkey and in the Middle East. This was a first test of physical stamina and strength for the nation, and it held its own, although almost 60,000 of the 330,000 troops perished in the war. A renewed patriotism cemented the country's confidence in itself. But, in the wake of so much slaughter, many Australians also questioned their relationship with their old colonial overlords. The bond between Britain and Australia was never quite the same again.

1441; www.roseofaustralia.com; 1 Swanson St; ⏱10am-10pm Sun & Mon, to midnight Tue-Sat; 🚉Erskineville)

Entertainment

Newtown Social Club   LIVE MUSIC

28 ⭐ Map p84, A7

The legendary Sandringham Hotel (aka the 'Sando', where God used to drink, according to local band the Whitlams) may have changed names but if anything it has heightened its commitment to live music. Gigs range from local bands on the make to indie luminaries such as Gruff Rhys and Stephen Malkmus. (📞1300 724 867; www.newtownsocialclub.com; 387 King St; ⏱7pm-midnight Tue-Thu, noon-2am Fri & Sat, noon-10pm Sun; ; 🚉Newtown)

Vanguard   LIVE MUSIC

29 ⭐ Map p84, C6

Intimate 1920s-themed Vanguard stages live music most nights (including some well-known names), as well as burlesque, comedy and classic-movie screenings. Most seats are reserved for dinner-and-show diners. (📞02-9557 7992; www.thevanguard.com.au; 42 King St; 🚉Macdonaldtown)

Enmore Theatre   LIVE MUSIC

30 ⭐ Map p84, A7

Originally a vaudeville playhouse, the elegantly wasted, 2500-capacity Enmore now hosts such acts as Paolo Nutini, Wilco and PJ Harvey, plus theatre, ballet and comedy. (📞02-9550 3666; www.enmoretheatre.com.au; 130 Enmore Rd; ⏱box office 9am-6pm Mon-Fri, 10am-4pm Sat; 🚉Newtown)

Understand
Literary Sydney

Australia's literary history harks back to Sydney's convict days. New experiences and landscapes inspired the colonists to commit their stories to the page. Though many early works have been lost, some – like Marcus Clarke's *For the Term of His Natural Life* (1870) – have become legendary.

By the late 19th century, a more formal Australian literary movement was developing with *The Bulletin,* an influential magazine promoting egalitarian and unionist thinking. Well-known contributing authors of the time included Henry Lawson (1867–1922) and AB 'Banjo' Paterson (1864–1941), who penned 'Waltzing Matilda'.

My Brilliant Career (1901), by Miles Franklin (1879–1954), is considered the first authentic Australian novel. The book caused a sensation when it was revealed that Miles was actually a woman.

Multi-award-winning Sydney authors of international stature include Patrick White (Nobel Prize in Literature, 1973), Thomas Keneally (Booker Prize winner, 1982), Peter Carey (Booker Prize winner 1988 and 2001) and Kate Grenville (Commonwealth Writers' Prize winner 2006). Other authors of note include David Malouf, Mandy Sayer, Shirley Hazzard, Eleanor Dark and Ruth Park.

Performance Space
PERFORMING ARTS

This edgy artists' hub stages performances of new dance, acrobatic and multimedia works – basically anything that can be lumped under the broad umbrella of 'the Arts'. Located at Carriageworks (see 3 ◉ Map p84, D6). (📞02-8571 9111; www.performancespace.com.au; Carriageworks, 245 Wilson St; 🚉Redfern)

Dendy Newtown
CINEMA

31 ⭐ Map p84, B6

Follow the buttery scent of popcorn into the dark folds of this plush cinema, screening first-run, independent world films. (📞02-9550 5699; www.dendy.com.au; 261 King St; adult/child $20/14; ⊙sessions 9.30am-9.30pm; 🚉Newtown)

New Theatre
THEATRE

32 ⭐ Map p84, B8

Australia's oldest continuously performing theatre (since 1932), Newtown's eclectic New Theatre produces new dramas as well as more established pieces. (📞02-9519 3403; www.newtheatre.org.au; 542 King St; tickets $17-32; 🚉St Peters)

Glebe Markets

Shopping

Glebe Markets MARKET

33 🔒 Map p84, D4

The best of the west; Sydney's dread-locked, shoeless, inner-city contingent beats a course to this crowded hippy-ish market. (www.glebemarkets.com.au; Glebe Public School, cnr Glebe Point Rd & Derby Pl; ⏱10am-4pm Sat; 🚊Glebe)

Gleebooks BOOKS

34 🔒 Map p84, D4

Generally regarded as Sydney's best bookshop, Gleebooks aisles are full of politics, arts and general fiction, and staff really know their stuff. Check their calendar for author talks and book launches. There's a separate secondhand store at 191 Glebe Point Rd. (☑02-9660 2333; www.gleebooks.com.au; 49 Glebe Point Rd; ⏱9am-7pm Sun-Wed, to 9pm Thu-Sat; 🚊Glebe)

Better Read Than Dead BOOKS

35 🔒 Map p84, B6

This just might be our favourite Sydney bookshop, and not just because of the pithy name and the great selection of Lonely Planet titles. Nobody seems to mind if you waste hours perusing the beautifully presented aisles, stacked with high-, middle- and deliciously low-brow reading materials. (☑02-9557

Gould's Book Arcade

8700; www.betterread.com.au; 265 King St; ⏱9.30am-9pm; 🚉Newtown)

Gould's Book Arcade   BOOKS

36 🔒 Map p84, C6

Possibly the world's scariest second-hand bookstore: the floor-to-ceiling racks and stacks threaten to bury you under a tonne of Stalinist analysis. All manner of musty out-of-print books are stocked, along with cassettes, records and even video tapes (VHS and Beta!). (☏02-9519 8947; www.goulds

books.com; 32 King St; ⏱10am-10.30pm; 🚉Macdonaldtown)

Faster Pussycat   CLOTHING, ACCESSORIES

37 🔒 Map p84, B8

Inspired by 'trash pop culture, hot rods and rock and roll', this cool cat coughs up clothing and accessories for all genders and ages (including baby punkwear) in several shades of Newtown black. (☏02-9519 1744; www.fasterpussycatonline.com; 431a King St; ⏱11am-6pm; 🚉Newtown)

Quick Brown Fox

CLOTHING, ACCESSORIES

38 🔒 Map p84, B6

No lazy dogs here – just plenty of fast-looking, tanned vixens snapping up funky vintage fashions that veer from 'hello, boys!' cuteness to indecent-exposure sexiness. Catchy patterns and fabrics, chic boots and bags. (☎02-9519 6622; www.quickbrownfox.com.au; 231 King St; ⏲10.30am-6.30pm; 🚈Newtown)

Reclaim

HOMEWARES, GIFTS

39 🔒 Map p84, B7

Absolutely the place to shop for Iggy Pop throw cushions, antique tea sets, quirky homewares and funky gifts. It's all put together by local singer Monica Trapaga (of Monica and the Moochers). (www.reclaim.net.au; 356 King St; ⏲10am-6pm; 🚈Newtown)

Deus Ex Machina

CLOTHING, ACCESSORIES

40 🔒 Map p84, B4

With a name translating to 'God is in the machine', this kooky showroom is crammed with classic and custom-made motorcycles and surfboards.

A hybrid workshop, cafe and offbeat boutique, it stocks men's and women's threads, including Deus-branded jeans, tees and shorts. (☎02-8594 2800; www.deuscustoms.com; 102-104 Parramatta Rd; ⏲9am-5pm; 🚌436-440)

Egg Records

MUSIC

41 🔒 Map p84, B7

There's something a bit too cool about this secondhand and new music store, but it's the perfect place to, say, complete your collection of 1980s David Bowie 12-inch singles, or pick up a Cramps T-shirt or a Gene Simmons figurine. (☎02-9550 6056; www.eggrecordsonline.com; 3 Wilson St; ⏲10am-6pm; 🚈Newtown)

Broadway Shopping Centre

SHOPPING CENTRE

42 🔒 Map p84, D4

Inside the rejuvenated Grace Bros building (check out the cool old globes above the facade), this centre has dozens of shops, a food court, a cinema complex and two supermarkets. (www.broadway.com.au; 1 Bay St; ⏲10am-7pm Fri-Wed, to 9pm Thu; 📶; 🚈Central)

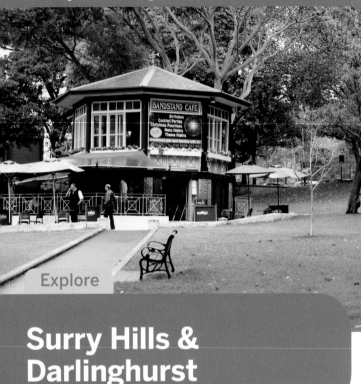

Explore

Surry Hills & Darlinghurst

Sydney's hippest and gayest neighbourhood is also home to its most interesting dining and bar scene. For the most part it's more gritty than pretty, and actual sights are thin on the ground, but there's still plenty to do and see here, especially after dark. Rows of Victorian terrace houses are a reminder of its working-class roots.

The Sights in a Day

☼ Spend most of the morning wandering around the **Australian Museum** (p100) and then take a long, leisurely walk to lunch at **Reuben Hills** (p110).

☀ After lunch, head up Albion St and wander through the heart of Surry Hills. Turn left on Bourke St to check out **Object Gallery** (p106) within the old St Margaret's Hospital complex. Head up to **Taylor Square** (p107), the hub of gay community life, and cross into Darlinghurst. Take Forbes St and cut through the **National Art School** (p104), stopping for a quick look around the gallery. Exiting on Burton St, turn right and continue to **Green Park** (p106). Spend the rest of the afternoon exploring the **Sydney Jewish Museum** (p104).

☾ Head out early and catch a cab to the **Devonshire** (p107); it offers an excellent pre-theatre deal. After dinner, if you haven't booked tickets for a play at **Belvoir** (p114) or a gig at the **Oxford Art Factory** (p114), take a stroll along Crown St. There are plenty of good bars and pubs to inspect along the way.

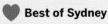

◉ **Top Sights**

Australian Museum (p100)

♥ **Best of Sydney**

Eating
Porteño (p108)

Bourke Street Bakery (p109)

Longrain (p109)

Bodega (p109)

Single Origin Roasters (p110)

Drinking
Wild Rover (p110)

Local Taphouse (p111)

Pocket (p111)

Hinky Dinks (p111)

The Winery (p112)

Beresford Hotel (p113)

121BC (p113)

Getting There

🚆 **Train** Apart from the very eastern fringe of Surry Hills, a train station is never more than a kilometre away. Exit at Museum for the blocks around Oxford St; Central for the rest of Surry Hills; and Kings Cross for the northern reaches of Darlinghurst.

🚌 **Bus** Numerous buses traverse Cleveland, Crown, Albion, Oxford, Liverpool and Flinders Sts.

Top Sights
Australian Museum

This natural-history museum, established just 40 years after the First Fleet dropped anchor, has endeavoured to shrug off its museum-that-should-be-in-a-museum feel by jazzing things up a little. Hence dusty taxidermy has been interspersed with video projections and a terrarium with live snakes, while dinosaur skeletons cosy up to life-size re-creations. Yet it's the most old-fashioned section that is arguably the most interesting – the hall of bones and the large collection of crystals and precious stones.

◉ Map p102, B1

☏ 02-9320 6000

www.australianmuseum.net.au

6 College St

adult/child $15/8

🕘 9.30am-5pm

🚇 Museum

iscover how they lived,
ed...and survived

Don't Miss

Surviving Australia

Exhibits simultaneously play up to tourists' fears of dangerous critters while cleverly contrasting this with information on animal extinctions. There are interesting displays on extinct megafauna such as the marsupial lion and giant wombat (simultaneously cuddly and terrifying). A sad 'where are they now' exhibit features stuffed remains and video footage of recently extinct species such as the Tasmanian tiger.

Indigenous Australians

This section covers Aboriginal history and spirituality, from Dreaming stories to the Freedom Rides of the 1960s, to contemporary issues – making good use of historical video clips and recorded testimonies along the way. A jail cell has a sobering account of Aboriginal deaths in custody, while political posters trace the history of the long battle for indigenous rights.

Skeletons

The fabulously macabre hall of bones, near the main entrance, has an intriguingly bizarre tableau of a skeletal man riding a horse. On the other wall, Skeletor sits in a comfy chair with his under-fed dog and a bird in a cage, while his cat chases a rat. Another bony bro has been made to look like he's riding a bicycle.

Minerals

In neighbouring halls on the first level, the Planet of Minerals and the Albert Chapman Mineral Collection house a fascinating array of colourful, glittering and implausibly shaped things that have been dug out of the earth and collected from caves. Check out the giant casts of actual gold nuggets found in Australia.

☑ **Top Tips**

▶ Special temporary exhibitions are held regularly and are charged separately.

▶ Once you've bought your ticket, it's possible to leave and re-enter the museum; pop out for a picnic in Hyde Park.

▶ Children under five get in for free.

▶ Kidspace on level 2 is a mini-museum for the under-fives.

✕ **Take a Break**

Just down the hill from the museum, **Bar Reggio** (Map p102, C1; ☎02-9332 1129; www.barreggio.com.au; 135 Crown St; mains $13-28; ⏱noon-11pm Mon-Sat; ▨; ▨Museum) is a remnant of a tiny Italian enclave centred on Stanley St. Its humble pasta, pizza and grills have stood the test of time.

The museum has its own cafe, located on Level 4.

MOORE PARK

Kippax Lagoon

Moore Park Rd

Gregory Ave

Anzac Pde

Sydney Boys & Girls High Schools

Cleveland St

Moore Park

Greens Rd

Iris St

Selwyn St

Josephson St

Flinders St

Hutchinson St

Nichols St

Fitzroy St

Fitzroy Pl

Fitzroy St

SURRY HILLS

Foveaux St

Riley St

Griffith St

Norton St

Collins La

Arthur St

Lacey St

Little Riley St

Adelaide St

Devonshire St

Ward Park

Marlborough St

Belvoir St

Riley St

Goodlet La

Goodlet St

Wilton St

Cleveland St

Baptist St

Chelsea St

Cisdell St

James St

Elizabeth St

Great Buckingham St

Buckingham St

Chalmers La

Chalmers St

Sophia St

Kippax St

Cooper St

Holt St

Hart St

Butt St

Waterloo St

Randle St

Bennett St

Fred Miller Park

Phelps St

Prospect St

Rainford St

Davies St

Raper St

Brett Whiteley Studio

Nickson St

Wilshire St

Crown St

Bourke St

Arthur St

Nobbs St

Parkham St

Mort St

Ridge St

South Dowling St

400 m
0.25 miles

20

11

44

9

12

28

16

33

29

10

13

3

26

8

6

Sights

Sydney Jewish Museum

MUSEUM

1 ◎ Map p102, E3

Created largely as a Holocaust memorial, this museum examines Australian Jewish history, culture and tradition, from the time of the First Fleet (which included 16 known Jews), to the immediate aftermath of WWII (when Australia became home to the greatest number of Holocaust survivors per capita, after Israel), to the present day. Allow at least two hours to take it all in. Free 45-minute tours leave at noon on Monday, Wednesday, Friday and Sunday. (☏02-9360 7999; www.sydney jewishmuseum.com.au; 148 Darlinghurst Rd; adult/child $10/7; ⏱10am-4pm Sun-Thu, to 2pm Fri; ☒Kings Cross)

National Art School

HISTORIC SITE, GALLERY

2 ◎ Map p102, D3

From 1841 to 1912 these sandstone buildings were Darlinghurst Gaol: writer Henry Lawson was incarcerated here several times for debt (he called the place 'Starvinghurst'). If today's art students think they've got it tough, they should spare a thought for the 732 prisoners who were crammed in here, or the 76 who were hanged. (www.nas.edu.au; Forbes St; admission free; ⏱gallery 11am-5pm Mon-Sat; ☒Kings Cross)

Sydney Jewish Museum

BOSILJKA ZUTICH / ALAMY ©

Understand

Aboriginal Australia

Origins & Culture

Australian Aboriginal society has the longest continuous cultural history in the world, its origins dating back to at least the last ice age. Aboriginal people were traditionally tribal, living in extended family groups. Knowledge obtained over millennia enabled them to use their environment extensively and sustainably; intimate knowledge of animal behaviour and plant harvesting ensured food shortages were rare.

Aboriginal Sydney

Governor Arthur Phillip estimated that around 1500 Aboriginal people lived around Sydney at first contact. The local people were known as the Eora (which literally means 'from this place'), broken into three main language groups and smaller clans such as the Gadigal and the Wangal.

Dispossession

As Aboriginal society was based on tribal family groups, a coordinated response to the European colonisers wasn't possible. The British declared Australia to be *terra nullius* (meaning 'land belonging to no one') and claimed it as their own. Some Aboriginal people were driven away, some were killed, many were shifted onto government reserves and missions, and thousands succumbed to European diseases.

From 1910 to the end of the 1960s, a policy of cultural assimilation allowed Aboriginal children to be forcibly removed from their families and schooled in the ways of white society. Around 100,000 children (dubbed the 'stolen generation') were separated from their parents in this way.

Seeds of Change

In 1967 a national referendum was held on whether to allow Aboriginal people the right to vote, which was passed by 90% of eligible voters. In 1992 a landmark High Court case overturned the principle of *terra nullius*, and in a later court case the Wik decision declared that pastoral leases do not necessarily extinguish native title, and that Aboriginal people could still claim ancestral land under white ownership. The implications of this ruling are still being resolved.

Brett Whiteley Studio

GALLERY

3 ⊙ Map p102, C6

Acclaimed local artist Brett Whiteley (1939–92) lived fast and without restraint. His hard-to-find studio (look for the signs on Devonshire St) has been preserved as a gallery for some of his best work. At the door is a miniature of his famous sculpture *Almost Once,* which you can see in all its glory in the Domain. (☏1800 679 278; www. brettwhiteley.org; 2 Raper St; admission free; ⊙10am-4pm Fri-Sun; ☒Central)

Object Gallery

GALLERY

4 ⊙ Map p102, C4

Inside the cylindrical former St Margaret's Hospital chapel (a 1958 modernist classic by architect Ken Woolley), nonprofit Object presents innovative exhibitions of new craft and design from Australia and overseas. Furniture, fashion, textiles and glass festoon three levels. (☏02-9361 4511; www.object.com.au; 415 Bourke St; admission free; ⊙11am-5pm Wed-Sat; ☒Central)

Green Park

PARK

5 ⊙ Map p102, D3

Once the residence of Alexander Green, hangman of Darlinghurst Gaol, Green Park is a cheery space during the day, but as the many syringe-disposal bins attest, it's best avoided nocturnally. At the top of the slope, the inverted pink triangular prism backed by black pillars is the Gay & Lesbian Holocaust Memorial. (cnr Victoria & Burton Sts; ☒Kings Cross)

Understand

World War II

In the years before WWII, Australia became increasingly fearful of the threat to national security posed by expansionist Japan. When war broke out, Australian troops again fought beside the British in Europe. Only after the Japanese bombed Pearl Harbor did Australia's own national security begin to take priority. A boom with a net barrage to prevent submarine access was stretched across the entrance channels of Sydney Harbour, and gun fortifications were set up on rocky harbour headlands.

Unlike the Northern Territory's capital city, Darwin, which was pretty much razed by Japanese bombings, Sydney escaped WWII virtually unscathed – although on 31 May 1942 three Japanese M24 midget submarines entered Sydney Harbour, sank a small supply vessel and lobbed a few shells into the suburbs of Bondi and Rose Bay.

Ultimately, the US victory in the Battle of the Coral Sea protected Australia from Japanese invasion and accelerated Australia's shift of allegiance from mother Britain to the USA.

Understand
Sydney's Housing Woes

If Sydneysiders seem utterly obsessed by real estate, it's for good reason. A 2012 Demographia survey rated Sydney as the third least affordable city (behind Vancouver and Hong Kong) in which to buy a house within the English-speaking world. Median house prices ($812,000) are 9.8 times higher than median household incomes ($82,800) – a ratio of 3:1 is considered affordable, above 5:1 severely unaffordable.

The silver lining? In most surveys of the world's most liveable cities, Sydney rates in the top 10.

Taylor Square
SQUARE

6 Map p102, D3

You know it's been a rough night if you wake up in Taylor Sq – a vaguely defined paved area straddling the gay hub of Oxford St. The stern Greek Revival Darlinghurst Courthouse (1842) watches the goings-on, no doubt disapprovingly. (cnr Oxford & Bourke Sts; Museum)

St John's Church
CHURCH

7 Map p102, E2

Grab a pamphlet inside this lovely sandstone church (1858) for an interesting 10-minute, self-guided tour. It makes for a hushed escape from the urban jangle of Darlinghurst Rd and the car wash next door. The Anglican congregation runs the Rough Edges Community Centre, working with the area's many homeless. (02-9360 6844; www.stjohnsanglican.org.au; 120 Darlinghurst Rd; 10am-2pm Mon-Fri; Kings Cross)

Moore Park
PARK

8 Map p102, D7

Part of the broader Centennial Parklands (a huge green swathe that cuts from Surry Hills to Bondi), Moore Park covers 115 hectares south of Paddington. With sports fields, tennis courts, an 18-hole public golf course and a site for visiting circuses, there's plenty here to keep you off the streets. (02-9339 6699; www.centennialparklands.com.au; Anzac Pde; Central)

Eating

Devonshire
MODERN EUROPEAN $$$

9 Map p102, B6

It's a long way from a two-Michelin-starred Mayfair restaurant to grungy old Devonshire St for chef Jeremy Bentley, although cuisinewise, perhaps not as far as you'd think. His food is simply extraordinary – complex, precisely presented and full of flavour. And while there's white linen on the tables, the atmosphere isn't the least bit starchy. (02-9698 9427; www.thedevonshire.com.au; 204 Devonshire St; mains $37; noon-2.30pm Fri, 6-10pm Tue-Sat; Central)

Porteño
ARGENTINE $$

 10   Map p102, B7

Lamb and suckling pig are spit-roasted for eight hours before the doors even open at this acclaimed and extremely hip restaurant, devoted to the robust meatiness of Argentinian cuisine. Arrive early to avoid a lengthy wait, although there's no hardship in hanging out upstairs at the very cool Gardel's Bar until a table comes free. (02-8399 1440; www.porteno.com.au; 358 Cleveland St; sharing plates $15-48; 6pm-midnight Tue-Sat; Central)

4Fourteen
MODERN AUSTRALIAN $$$

11   Map p102, C5

When he's not busy terrorising contestants on TV cooking shows, Irish-born chef Colin Fassnidge can be found cranking out hearty, meaty dishes at one of his Sydney eateries, the newest of which is this big, fun buzzy place. Solo diners should grab a seat by the kitchen for dinner with a show. (02-9331 5399; www.4fourteen.com.au; 414 Bourke St; mains $30-42; noon-3pm Tue-Sun, 6-11pm Tue-Sat; Central)

Devon
CAFE $$

12   Map p102, A5

If it's boring old bacon and eggs you're after, look elsewhere. Devon shamelessly plunders the cuisines of 'multicultural Australia' to deliver an extremely creative menu, with plenty of twists on old favourites.

STACEY FISHER / IMAGE COURTESY OF BOURKE STREET BAKERY

Bourke Street Bakery

There's even an 'Ogre's Happy Meal' (ox-tongue, apparently – we weren't tempted). (www.devoncafe.com.au; 76 Devonshire St; mains $14-21; ⏰7am-4.30pm daily, 6-10pm Thu-Sat)

Bourke Street Bakery BAKERY $

13 ✕ Map p102, C7

Queuing outside this teensy bakery is an essential Surry Hills experience. It sells a tempting selection of pastries, cakes, bread and sandwiches, along with sausage rolls which are near legendary in these parts. There are a few tables inside but on a fine day you're better off on the street. (www. bourkestreetbakery.com.au; 633 Bourke St; items $5-14; ⏰8am-5pm; 🚇Central)

Longrain THAI $$

14 ✕ Map p102, B3

Devotees flock to this century-old, wedge-shaped printing-press building to feast on fragrant modern Thai dishes, and to sip delicately flavoured and utterly delicious cocktails. Sit at shared tables or at the bar. (☎02-9280 2888; www.longrain.com; 85 Commonwealth St; mains $18-38; ⏰noon-2.30pm Fri, 6-11pm daily; 🚇Central)

Bodega TAPAS $$

15 ✕ Map p102, B4

The coolest progeny of Sydney's tapas explosion, Bodega has a casual vibe, good-lookin' staff and a funky matador mural. Dishes vary widely in size and

There's Black Gold in Them There Hills

Coffee seekers won't need to dig deep to find great brews in this neighbourhood. For a seriously good buzz, head to either **Sample Coffee** (www.samplecoffee.com.au; 118 Devonshire St; items $3-5; ⏰6.30am-4pm Mon-Fri; Ⓡ Central) or **Single Origin Roasters** (📞02-9211 0665; www.singleorigin.com.au; 60-64 Reservoir St; mains $13-17; ⏰6.30am-4pm Mon-Fri; Ⓡ Central); both are contenders for the top gong. To rub shoulders with the locals, head to grungy **fourate-five** (www.fouratefive.com; 485 Crown St; mains $10-19; ⏰7am-3.30pm Mon-Sat, 9.30am-2.30pm Sun; 📷; Ⓡ Central) or tiny, wedge-shaped **Pablo's Vice** (www.facebook.com/pablosvice; 3/257 Crown St; mains $7-15; ⏰7am-4.30pm Mon-Sat; Ⓡ Museum).

price. Wash 'em down with Spanish and South American wine, sherry, port or beer, and plenty of Latin gusto. (📞02-9212 7766; www.bodegatapas.com; 216 Commonwealth St; tapas $12-28; ⏰noon-2pm Fri, 6-10pm Tue-Sat; Ⓡ Central)

MoVida
SPANISH $$

16 Map p102, A6

A Sydney incarnation of a Melbourne legend, MoVida serves top-notch tapas and *raciones* (larger shared plates), and a great selection of Spanish wines. Book well ahead for a table or get in early for a seat by the bar. (📞02-8964

7642; www.movida.com.au; 50 Holt St; tapas $5-13, raciones $17-26, mains $29; ⏰noon-late Mon-Sat; Ⓡ Central)

Messina
ICE CREAM $

17 Map p102, E2

Join the queues of people who look like they never eat ice cream at the counter of Sydney's most popular gelato shop. Clearly even the beautiful people can't resist quirky flavours such as figs in Marsala and salted caramel. The attached dessert bar serves sundaes. (www.gelatomessina.com; 241 Victoria St; 2 scoops $6; ⏰noon-11pm; Ⓡ Kings Cross)

Reuben Hills
CAFE $

18 Map p102, B4

An industrial fitout and Latin American menu await at Reuben Hills (aka hipster central). Fantastic single-origin coffee and fried chicken, but the eggs, tacos and *baleadas* (Honduran tortillas) are no slouches, either. (www.reubenhills. com.au; 61 Albion St; mains $12-18; ⏰7am-4pm; 📶; Ⓡ Central)

Drinking

Wild Rover
BAR

19 Map p102, A3

Look for the old sign on the window reading 'Gestetner's Surry Hills Shirt Warehouse' and enter this supremely cool brick-lined speakeasy, where a big range of craft beer is served in chrome steins. Live bands play upstairs a couple of nights a week. (www.thewildrover.com.au; 75 Campbell St; ☺4pm-midnight Mon-Sat, to 10pm Sun; 圓Central)

Local Taphouse

PUB

20 🚇 Map p102, D5

Beer lovers can test their palates against the tasting notes as they work their way through dozens of craft beers at this angular old pub. There aren't any views but the little high-sided rooftop is a great spot to catch the breeze. (www.thelocal.com.au; 122 Flinders St; ☺noon-midnight; 🚌396-399)

Pocket

BAR

21 🚇 Map p102, C2

Sink into the corner Pocket's comfy leather couches, order a drink from one of the cheery waitstaff, and chat about the day's adventures over a decade-defying indie soundtrack. Pop-art murals and exposed brickwork add to the underground ambience. (www.pocketsydney.com.au; 13 Burton St; ☺4pm-midnight; 圓Museum)

Hinky Dinks

COCKTAIL BAR

22 🚇 Map p102, E1

Everything's just hunky dory in this little cocktail bar styled after a 1950s milkshake parlour. Try the Hinky Fizz, an alcohol-soaked strawberry sorbet served in a waxed paper sundae cup. (www.hinkydinks.com.au; 185 Darlinghurst Rd; ☺1-10pm Sun, 4pm-midnight Mon-Sat; 圓Kings Cross)

Understand
Sydney Mardi Gras

Sydney's famous **Gay & Lesbian Mardi Gras** (www.mardigras.org.au) is now the biggest annual tourist-attracting date on the Australian calendar. While the straights focus on the parade, the gay and lesbian community throws itself wholeheartedly into the entire festival, including the blitzkrieg of partying that surrounds it. There's no better time for the gay traveller to visit Sydney than the two-week lead-up to the parade and party, held on the first Saturday in March.

On the big night itself, the parade kicks off around sunset, preceded by the throbbing engines of hundreds of Dykes on Bikes. Heading up Oxford St from Hyde Park, it veers right into Flinders St, hooking into Moore Park Rd and culminating outside the party site in Driver Ave. The whole thing takes about 90 minutes to trundle through, and attracts hundreds of thousands of spectators ogling from the sidelines.

The parade has a serious political bent, commemorating a 1978 gay rights march that ended in participants being arrested and beaten.

Local Life

Darlinghurst's Gay Scene

The **Stonewall Hotel** (☏02-9360 1963; www.stonewallhotel.com; 175 Oxford St; ⏱noon-3am; ☒Museum) has three levels of bars and dance floors, and attracts a younger crowd. **Midnight Shift** (☏02-9358 3848; www.themidnightshift.com.au; 85 Oxford St; admission free-$10; ⏱4pm-late Thu-Sun; ☒Museum) is the grand dame of the scene, known for the lavish drag productions in its upstairs nightclub. In subterranean **Palms on Oxford** (☏02-9357 4166; 124 Oxford St; ⏱8pm-1am Thu & Sun, to 3am Fri & Sat; ☒Museum), the 1980s lives on. Serious clubbers head to **Arq** (www.arqsydney.com.au; 16 Flinders St; ⏱9pm-5am Thu & Sun, 9pm-noon Fri & Sat; ☒Museum).

Shady Pines Saloon BAR

23 🚇 Map p102, C3

With no sign or street number on the door and entry via a shady back lane (look for the white door before Bikram Yoga on Foley St), this subterranean honky-tonk bar caters to the urban boho. Sip whisky and rye with the good ole hipster boys amid Western memorabilia and taxidermy. (www.shadypinessaloon.com; shop 4, 256 Crown St; ⏱4pm-midnight; ☒Museum)

The Winery WINE BAR

24 🚇 Map p102, C4

Set back from the road in the leafy grounds of a historic water reservoir, this wine bar serves dozens of wines by the glass to the swankier Surry Hills set. Sit for a while and you'll notice all kinds of kitsch touches lurking in the greenery: headless statues, upside-down parrots, iron koalas. (www.thewinerysurryhills.com.au; 285a Crown St; ⏱noon-midnight; ☒Museum)

Tio's Cerveceria BAR

25 🚇 Map p102, B3

Tio likes tequila. Heaps of different types. And wrestling, Catholic kitsch and *Day of the Dead* paraphernalia. Surry Hills skaters, beard-wearers and baby-doll babes love him right back. (4-14 Foster St; ⏱5pm-midnight; ☒Museum)

Vasco COCKTAIL BAR

26 🚇 Map p102, C8

Like the much, much hipper and better-looking Italian cousin of a Hard Rock Cafe, Vasco serves beer, wine and rock-themed cocktails in a room lined with band photos and guitars. Order a plate of *salumi* or pasta to snack on as you sip your Monkey Gone to Heaven, while Jagger sneers on the screen. (www.vascobar.com; 421 Cleveland St; ⏱5pm-midnight Tue-Sat; 372)

PETER SEDLÁČEK / IMAGE COURTESY OF SLIDE

A Risqué Revue burlesque show at Slide

Beresford Hotel PUB

27 🚇 Map p102, C4

The once-grungy Beresford (circa 1870) has turned into a superslick architectural tractor beam designed to reel in the beautiful people. The crowd will make you feel either inadequate or right at home, depending on how the mirror is treating you. There's a vast new beer garden, and upstairs is a schmick live-music/club space. (www.merivale.com.au/theberesfordhotel; 354 Bourke St; ☉noon-midnight; 🚉Central)

121BC WINE BAR

28 🚇 Map p102, A5

The first challenge is finding it (enter from Gladstone St) and the second is scoring a table. After that, it's easy – seat yourself at the communal table under the bubbly light fixture and ask the waitstaff to suggest delicious drops and snacks to suit your inclinations. Everything's good, so you can't really go wrong. (www.121bc.com.au; 4/50 Holt St; ☉5pm-midnight Tue-Sat; 🚉Central)

Entertainment

Belvoir   THEATRE

29 ⭐ Map p102, A7

In a quiet corner of Surry Hills, this intimate venue is the home of an often-experimental and consistently excellent theatre company. Shows sometimes feature big stars. (☎02-9699 3444; www.belvoir.com.au; 25 Belvoir St; 🚉Central)

SBW Stables Theatre   THEATRE

30 ⭐ Map p102, E2

In the 19th century this place was knee-high in horse dung; now it's home to the Griffin Theatre Company, dedicated to nurturing new Australian writers. It's also where many actors started out – Cate Blanchett and David Wenham both trod the boards here. Monday Rush tickets (two for $20) are available for certain performances. (☎02-9361 3817; www.griffintheatre.com.au; 10 Nimrod St; 🚉Kings Cross)

Eternity Playhouse   THEATRE

31 ⭐ Map p102, C3

Based in a beautifully restored Baptist tabernacle (1887), the Darlinghurst Theatre Company focuses on bringing pithy, intelligent Australian scripts to the stage. (☎02-8356 9987; www.darlinghursttheatre.com; 39 Burton St; 🚉Museum)

Oxford Art Factory   LIVE MUSIC

32 ⭐ Map p102, C2

Indie kids party against an arty backdrop at this two-room multipurpose venue modelled on Andy Warhol's NYC creative base. There's a gallery, a bar and a performance space that often hosts international acts and DJs. Check the website for what's on. (www.oxfordartfactory.com; 38-46 Oxford St; 🚉Museum)

Venue 505   LIVE MUSIC

33 ⭐ Map p102, A7

Focusing on jazz, roots, reggae, funk, gypsy and Latin music, this small, relaxed venue is artist-run and thoughtfully programmed. The space features comfortable couches and murals by a local artist. (www.venue505.com; 280 Cleveland St; ⊙doors open 6pm Mon-Sat; 🚉Central)

Slide   CABARET

34 ⭐ Map p102, B2

Slide inside a gorgeously converted banking chamber for dinner and a sexy show: cabaret, circus, burlesque etc. (☎02-8915 1899; www.slide.com.au; 41 Oxford St; ⊙7pm-late Wed-Sat; 🚉Museum)

Govinda's   CINEMA

35 ⭐ Map p102, E2

The Hare Krishna Govinda's is an all-you-can-gobble vegetarian smorgasbord, including admission to the movie

---

Understand
Paddington Fashion

For several decades Paddington, Darlinghurst's eastern neighbour, has held the reputation of being Sydney's premier fashion 'hood. While it's taken a hit in recent years with the opening of the fabulously upmarket and oversized Westfield Bondi Junction (p66) shopping mall just up the road, Paddington's Oxford St, William St and Glenmore Rd are still dotted with signature stores for many of the leading names in Australian fashion – **Leona Edmiston** (www.leonaedmiston.com; 88 William St; ⏰noon-6pm Sun-Tue, 10am-6pm Wed-Sat; 🚌380), **Sass & Bide** (www.sassandbide.com; 132 Oxford St; ⏰10am-6pm Fri-Wed, to 8pm Thu; 🚌380) and **Scanlan Theodore** (📞02-9380 9388; www.scanlantheodore.com.au; 122 Oxford St; 🚌380) among them.

Interesting little boutiques include **Capital L** (📞02-9361 0111; www.capital-l.com; 100 Oxford St; ⏰10.30am-6pm; 🚉Kings Cross), which features the work of up-and-coming Australian designers. **Corner Shop** (📞02-9380 9828; www.thecornershop.com.au; 43 William St; ⏰10am-6pm Mon-Sat, noon-5pm Sun; 🚌380) and **Poepke** (www.poepke.com; 47 William St; ⏰10am-6pm Mon-Sat, noon-5pm Sun; 🚌380) carry a curated selection of local and international brands.

---

room upstairs. Expect blockbusters, art-house classics, incense in the air and cushions on the floor. (📞02-9380 5155; www.govindas.com.au; 112 Darlinghurst Rd; dinner & movie $30, movie only $16; ⏰Wed-Sat; 🚉Kings Cross)

Shopping

Blue Spinach
FASHION

36 Map p102, E2

High-end consignment clothing for penny-pinching label lovers of all genders. If you can make it beyond the shocking blue facade (shocking doesn't really do it justice), you'll find Paul Smith and Gucci at (relatively) bargain prices. (📞02-9331 3904; www.bluespinach.com.au; 348 Liverpool St; 🚉Kings Cross)

Artery
ARTS

37 🔒 Map p102, E2

Step into a world of mesmerising dots and swirls at this small gallery devoted to Aboriginal art. Artery's motto is 'ethical, contemporary, affordable', and while large canvases by more established artists cost in the thousands, small, unstretched canvases start at around $35. (📞02-9380 8234; www.artery.com.au; 221 Darlinghurst Rd; ⏰10am-6pm Mon-Fri, to 4pm Sat & Sun; 🚉Kings Cross)

Workshopped

GIFTS

38 🔒 Map p102, D4

The work of Australian designers is showcased in this funky little store, which focuses on practical but beautiful things for the home: ceramics, wood, soft furnishings etc. (www.workshopped.com.au; 2/8 Hill St; ⏱10am-5pm Mon-Sat; 🚌374-6)

Holy Kitsch!

GIFTS

39 🔒 Map p102, C4

When you've a hole that only Day of the Dead and Mexican wrestling paraphernalia can fill, come here. There's another branch in **Newtown** (4 Enmore Rd; ⏱noon-6pm; 🚊Newtown). (www.holykitsch.com.au; 321 Crown St; ⏱10.30am-6pm Wed-Mon; 🚊Central)

Wheels & Dollbaby

CLOTHING

40 🔒 Map p102, C3

'Clothes to Snare a Millionaire' is the name of the game here, and what a wicked, wicked game it is: lace, leather and leopard print; studs, suspenders and satin. Tight wrapped and trussed up; it won't just be the millionaires who'll be looking your way. Male rockers will have to settle for T-shirts. (☎02-9361 3286; www.wheelsanddollbaby.com; 259 Crown St; ⏱10am-6pm Fri-Wed, to 8pm Thu; 🚊Museum)

Bookshop Darlinghurst

BOOKS

41 🔒 Map p102, D3

This outstanding bookshop specialises in gay and lesbian tomes, with everything from queer crime and lesbian fiction to glossy pictorials and porn. A diverting browse, to say the least (hmm…which would look better on my coffee table: the *Big Book of Breasts* or the *Big Penis Book*?). (☎02-9331 1103; www.thebookshop.com.au; 207 Oxford St; ⏱10am-7pm Sun-Wed, to 9pm Thu-Sat; 🚊Kings Cross)

House of Priscilla

CLOTHING, ACCESSORIES

42 🔒 Map p102, C2

Not only is Priscilla the queen of the desert, she also has her own boutique – not bad for a cinematic bus. Run by some of the city's leading drag artistes, Priscilla is the place for feathered angel wings, naughty nurse outfits, Beyoncé wigs, kinky thigh-high boots and sequinned frocks to fit front-row forwards. Very camp women also welcome. (☎02-9286 3023; www.houseofpriscilla.com.au; Level 1, 47 Oxford St; ⏱10am-6pm Mon-Wed, Fri & Sat, to 8pm Thu; 🚊Museum)

Sax Fetish

CLOTHING, ADULT

43 🔒 Map p102, C3

No, it's not a bar for jazz obsessives, but rather a sexy, dark-hearted shop selling high-quality leather and rubber

Sass & Bide (p115)

gear. All genders are catered for, and the 'accessories' range goes a little further than your standard belts and handbags (cufflinks and ties take on a whole new meaning here). (☎02-9331 6105; www.saxfetish.com; 110a Oxford St; ⏱11am-7pm; ◪Museum)

Surry Hills Markets
MARKET

44 🔒 Map p102, C5

There's a chipper community vibe at this monthly market, with mainly locals renting stalls to sell/recycle their old stuff: clothes, CDs, books and sundry junk. Bargains aplenty. (www. shnc.org/events/surry-hills-markets; Shannon Reserve, Crown St; ⏱7am-4pm 1st Sat of month; ◪Central)

C's Flashback
VINTAGE

45 🔒 Map p102, C3

Looking for a secondhand Hawaiian shirt, some beat-up cowboy boots or a little sequinned 1940s hat like the Queen wears? We're not sure exactly what C was on, but her flashback men's and women's threads are pretty trippy. (☎02-9331 7833; www.csflashback. com.au; 316 Crown St; ⏱10am-6pm Fri-Wed, to 8pm Thu; ◪Museum)

Local Life
A Saturday in Paddington

Getting There

🚌 Routes 378 (Railway Sq to Bronte) and 380 (Circular Quay to Watsons Bay via Bondi) head along Oxford St. Route 389 (Circular Quay to Bondi) takes the back roads.

Paddington is an elegant neighbourhood of restored terrace houses and steep leafy streets where fashionable folks (seemingly without the need to occupy an office) drift between boutiques, art galleries and bookshops. The suburb's pulsing artery is Oxford St, built over an ancient track used by the Gadigal people. The liveliest time to visit is on Saturday, when the markets are effervescing.

❶ Hang out in Five Ways

Oxford St may be the main drag, but the quirky cafes, galleries, shops and pub at the star-like junction of Five Ways make it the hip heart of Paddington. Start with coffee in **Sonoma** (www.sonoma.com.au; 241 Glenmore Rd; mains $6-18; ⏱7am-3pm; 🚍389), a bakery-cafe specialising in sourdough bread and popular with the yummy-mummy set.

❷ Peer at Victoria Barracks

A manicured vision from the peak of the British Empire, these Georgian **barracks** (📞02-8335 5170; www.armymuseumnsw.com.au; Oxford St; admission free; ⏱tours 10am Thu; 🚍380), built 1841–48, have been called the finest of their kind in the colonies. They're still part of an army base, so unless you return for the tour you'll have to peer through the gates.

❸ Stroll Through Paddington Reservoir Gardens

Opened to much architectural acclaim in 2008, this impressive **park** (cnr Oxford St & Oatley Rd; 🚍380) makes use of Paddington's long-abandoned 1866 water reservoir, incorporating the brick arches and surviving chamber into an interesting green space featuring a sunken garden, pond, boardwalk and lawns. They've even preserved some of the graffiti.

❹ Visit the Australian Centre for Photography

The nonprofit **ACP** (ACP; 📞02-9332 0555; www.acp.org.au; 257 Oxford St; admission free; ⏱10am-5pm Tue-Sat, noon-5pm Sun; 🚍380) exhibits the photographic gems of renowned Sydney and international photographers. It's particularly passionate about photomedia, video and digital-imaging works. Exhibitions change regularly and the busy calendar includes talks, screenings and other events.

❺ Experience Paddington Markets

A cultural experience, these quirky, long-running markets turn Saturdays in Paddington into pandemonium. In the 1970s, when they started, **Paddington Markets** (www.paddingtonmarkets.com.au; 395 Oxford St; ⏱10am-4pm Sat; 🚍380) were distinctly countercultural. It's a tad more mainstream now, but still worth checking out for new and vintage clothing, creative crafts, jewellery, food, palm-reading and holistic treatments.

❻ Explore Centennial Park

Scratched out of the sand in 1888 in grand Victorian style, Sydney's biggest **park** (📞02-9339 6699; www.centennialparklands.com.au; Oxford St; 🚉Bondi Junction) is a rambling 189-hectare expanse full of horse riders, joggers, cyclists and in-line skaters. Among the wide formal avenues, ponds and statues is the domed Federation Pavilion – the spot where Australia was officially proclaimed a nation.

Explore

Kings Cross & Potts Point

If Darling Harbour is Sydney dressing up nicely for tourists, the Cross is where it relaxes, scratches itself and belches. In equal parts thrilling and depressing but never boring, this is the go-to zone for late-night blinders. In gracious, tree-lined Potts Point and Elizabeth Bay, well-preserved Victorian, Edwardian and art deco houses flank picturesque streets.

The Sights in a Day

Start your day with breakfast at **Room 10** (p127). Take a stroll along Darlinghurst Rd, reading the bronze social history plaques set into the footpath along the way. The El Alamein Fountain marks the beginning of **Fitzroy Gardens** (p125); stop to rummage through the weekend markets. Continue down to Elizabeth Bay and spend the rest of the morning in **Elizabeth Bay House** (p125). Wander up the stairs near 17 Billyard Ave and head to **Fratelli Paradiso** (p127) for lunch.

Continue along Challis Ave, admiring the impressive row of colonnaded mansions. At the end, there's a great view over Woolloomooloo from Embarkation Park. Turn left and stroll along leafy Victoria St. If you're planning a big night, head back to your accommodation for a pre-disco nap. Otherwise, while away the afternoon on the rooftop of the **Kings Cross Hotel** (p128).

Grab dinner at **Ms G's** (p126) and then hit the bars and clubs.

For a local's day in Kings Cross & Potts Point, see p122.

Local Life

Wandering Around Woolloomooloo (p122)

Best of Sydney

Eating
Cho Cho San (p126)

Historic Buildings
Elizabeth Bay House (p125)

Markets
Fitzroy Gardens (p125)

Getting There

🚃 **Train** Everywhere is within walking distance of Kings Cross station, although the western fringe of Woolloomooloo is closer to St James.

🚌 **Bus** Route 311 hooks through Kings Cross, Potts Point, Elizabeth Bay and Woolloomooloo on its circuitous route from Railway Sq. Buses 324 and 325 (Circular Quay–Watsons Bay) pass through Bayswater Rd in Kings Cross.

Local Life
Wandering Around Woolloomooloo

Squeezed between the Domain and Kings Cross, Woolloomooloo (show us another word with eight Os!) is a suburb in transition. Once solidly working class, it still has some rough edges, but down by the water they're hard to spot. The navy base is still here, but drunken sailors are in short supply.

....

❶ **Descend McElhone Stairs**

These stone **stairs** (Victoria St; 🚇 Kings Cross) were built in 1870 to connect spiffy Potts Point with the Woolloomooloo slums below. The steep steps run past an apartment block: residents sip tea on their balconies and stare bemusedly at the fitness freaks punishing themselves on the 113-stair uphill climb.

2 Snack at Harry's
Cafe de Wheels

Sure, it's a humble pie cart, but
Harry's (www.harryscafedewheels.com.au;
Cowper Wharf Rdwy; pies $5-7; ⊙9am-1am
Sun, 8.30am-3am Mon-Sat; ℝKings Cross)
is a tourist attraction nonetheless.
Open since 1938 (except when founder
Harry 'Tiger' Edwards was on active
service), Harry's has served the good
stuff to everyone from Pamela Ander-
son to Colonel Sanders.

3 Woolloomooloo Finger Wharf

A former wool and cargo dock, this
beautiful Edwardian wharf faced
oblivion for decades before a 2½-year
demolition-workers' green ban on
the site in the late 1980s saved it. It
received a huge sprucing up in the
late 1990s and has emerged as one of
Sydney's most exclusive eating, drinking, sleeping and marina addresses.

4 Relax in the Waterbar

After a few martinis in the heart
of Woolloomooloo's wharf, time
becomes meaningless and escape
pointless. Lofty, romantic **Waterbar**
(www.waterbaratblue.com; 6 Cowper Wharf
Rdwy; ⊙5-10pm Sun & Mon, to midnight
Tue-Sat; ℝKings Cross) sucks you in to
its pink-love world of deep lounges
and ottomans as big as beds. Great for
business, but better for lurve.

5 Space Out in Artspace

Artspace (☏02-9356 0555; www.artspace.
org.au; 43-51 Cowper Wharf Rd; admission
free; ⊙11am-5pm Tue-Sun; ℝKings Cross)
is spacey: its eternal quest is to fill the
void with vigorous, engaging contemporary art. Things here are decidedly
avant-garde – expect lots of concep-
tual pieces, audio visual installations
and new-media masterpieces. It's an
admirable attempt to liven things up
in Sydney's art scene.

6 Top up at Toby's Estate

Coffee is undoubtedly the main event
at this cool little charcoal-coloured
roastery, but **Toby's Estate** (☏02-9358
1196; www.tobysestate.com.au; 129 Cathedral
St; meals $10-15; ⊙7am-4pm; ☞; ℝSt
James) is also a great place for a quick
sandwich, a veggie wrap or a fat muf-
fin. And the caffeine? Strong, perfectly
brewed and usually fair trade.

7 Settle in at the Old Fitzroy

Islington meets Melbourne in the back
streets of Woolloomooloo: this totally
unpretentious theatre **pub** (www.old
fitzroy.com.au; 129 Dowling St; ⊙11am-
midnight Mon-Sat, 3-10pm Sun; ☞; ℝKings
Cross) is also a decent old-fashioned
boozer in its own right. Prop up the bar,
grab a seat outside or head upstairs to
the bistro, pool table and couches.

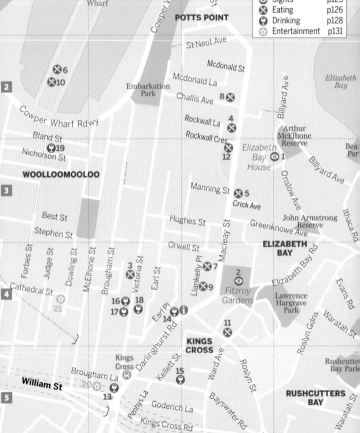

A   B   C   D

1

Woolloomooloo Bay

Woolloomooloo Finger Wharf

POTTS POINT

Cowper Wharf Rdwy

Wylde St

St Neot Ave

Mcdonald St

0   200 m
0   0.1 miles

For reviews see
- ⊙ Sights p125
- ⊗ Eating p126
- ⊖ Drinking p128
- ✷ Entertainment p131

2

⊗6
⊗10

Embarkation Park

Mcdonald La

Challis Ave   8⊗

Cowper Wharf Rdwy

Rockwall La   4
⊗

Rockwall Cres   ⊗
12

Billyard Ave

Elizabeth Bay

Arthur McElhone Reserve

Bea Par

Elizabeth Bay House   ⊙1

Billyard Ave

Bland St   ⊖19

Nicholson St

WOOLLOOMOOLOO

3

Best St

Stephen St

Manning St   ⊗5

Crick Ave

Hughes St

Macleay St

Greenknowe Ave

Onslow Ave

John Armstrong Reserve

ELIZABETH BAY

Elizabeth Bay Rd

Ithaca Rd

Orwell St

Llankelly Pl

7
⊗

Fitzroy Gardens

2
⊙

Lawrence Hargrave Park

Roslyn Gdns

Evans Rd

Waratah St

Forbes St

Judge St

Dowling St

McElhone St

Brougham St

Victoria St   3
⊗

Earl St

Earl Pl

4

Cathedral St   ✷
21

16⊖ 18
17⊖

14⊖   ❶

⊗9

KINGS CROSS

11
⊗

Ward Ave

Roslyn St

Rushcutte Bay Park

RUSHCUTTERS BAY

Waratah St

5

William St

Brougham La   ⊖
✷   13
20

Kings Cross

Darlinghurst Rd

Kellett St

15   ⊖

Penny's La

Goderich La

Kings Cross Rd

Bayswater Rd

Roslyn St

Sights

Elizabeth Bay House

HISTORIC BUILDING

1 Map p124, D3

Now dwarfed by 20th-century apartments, Colonial Secretary Alexander Macleay's elegant Greek Revival mansion was one of the finest houses in the colony when it was completed in 1839. The architectural highlight is an exquisite oval entrance saloon with a curved and cantilevered staircase. (02-9356 3022; www.sydneyliving museums.com.au; 7 Onslow Ave; adult/child $8/4; 11am-4pm Fri-Sun; Kings Cross)

Fitzroy Gardens

PARK

2 Map p124, C4

It's testimony to the 'cleaning up' of the Cross that this once-dodgy park is now a reasonably safe place to hang out (probably helped by the austere police station in the corner). It still feels seedy, though: malnourished seagulls compete for scraps with pigeons who look like Keith Richards, while bearded homeless guys compile cigarettes from discarded butts. (cnr Macleay St & Darlinghurst Rd; Kings Cross)

HOLGER LEUE / GETTY IMAGES ©

Elizabeth Bay House

Understand
Where Exactly Is Kings Cross?

Where exactly is Kings Cross? Although technically it's just the intersection of William and Victoria Sts (where the streets named after two kings cross; OK, so one's a queen, but let's not split hairs), in reality it's more of a mindset than an exact geographical place. What most people call Kings Cross falls within the suburb of Potts Point; businesses tend to use a Potts Point address if they want to sound classy and Kings Cross if they want to emphasise their party cred. Either way, you'll know Kings Cross when you see it.

Eating

Ms G's
ASIAN $$

 3 Map p124, B4

Offering a cheeky, irreverent take on Asian cooking (hence the name – geddit?), Ms G's is nothing if not an experience. It can be loud, frantic and painfully hip, but the adventurous combinations of pan-Asian and European flavours have certainly got Sydney talking. (☑02-9240 3000; www.merivale.com/msgs; 155 Victoria St; mains $25-38; ☉1-9pm Sun, noon-3pm Fri, 6-11pm Mon-Sat; ☒Kings Cross)

Cho Cho San
JAPANESE $$

4 Map p124, C2

Glide through the shiny brass sliding door and take a seat at the polished concrete communal table which runs the length of this stylish Japanese restaurant. The food is just as artful as the surrounds, with tasty *izakaya*-style bites emanating from both the raw bar and the *hibachi* grill. (☑02-9331 6601; www.chochosan.com.au;

73 Macleay St; mains $14-36; ☉noon-3pm Fri-Sun, 6-11pm daily; ☒Kings Cross)

Apollo
GREEK $$

 5 Map p124, C3

An exemplar of modern Greek cooking, this taverna has fashionably minimalist decor, a well-priced menu of share plates and a bustling vibe. Starters are particularly impressive, especially the pitta bread hot from the oven, the fried saganaki with honey and oregano, and the wild weed and cheese pie. (☑02-8354 0888; www.theapollo.com.au; 44 Macleay St; mains $26-34; ☉6-11pm Mon-Thu, noon-11pm Fri & Sat, noon-9.30pm Sun; ☒Kings Cross)

Otto Ristorante
ITALIAN $$$

 6 Map p124, A2

Forget the glamorous waterfront location and the A-list crowd – Otto will be remembered for single-handedly dragging Sydney's Italian cooking into the new century with dishes such as *strozzapreti con gamberi* (artisan pasta with fresh Yamba prawns, tomato, chilli and black olives). Bookings essential.

(☎02-9368 7488; www.ottoristorante.com.au; 8/6 Cowper Wharf Rdwy; mains $41-59; ⏱noon-3pm & 6-11pm; ☒Kings Cross)

Room 10
CAFE $

 7 Map p124, C4

If you're wearing a flat cap, sprouting a beard and obsessed by coffee, chances are you'll recognise this tiny room as your spiritual home in the Cross. The food's limited to sandwiches, salads and such – tasty and uncomplicated. (10 Llankelly Pl; mains $9-14; ⏱7am-4pm; ☒Kings Cross)

Fratelli Paradiso
ITALIAN $$

 8 Map p124, C2

This underlit trattoria has them queuing at the door (especially on weekends). The intimate room showcases seasonal Italian dishes cooked with Mediterranean zing. Lots of busy black-clad waiters, lots of Italian chatter, lots of oversized sunglasses. No bookings. (www.fratelli paradiso.com; 12-16 Challis Ave; breakfast $12-14, mains $22-31; ⏱7am-11pm; ☒Kings Cross)

Wilbur's Place
CAFE, BISTRO $$

 9 Map p124, C4

With limited bench seating inside and a few tables on the lane, tiny Wilbur's is an informal spot for a quick bite on what's become the Cross' coolest cafe strip. Expect simple, straightforward food that is expertly assembled. (www.wilbursplace.com; 36 Llankelly Pl; brunch $9-19, dinner $28; ⏱8am-3pm Sat, 5-9.30pm Tue-Sat; ☒Kings Cross)

China Doll
ASIAN $$$

 10 Map p124, A2

Gaze over the Woolloomooloo marina and city skyline as you tuck into

---

Understand
Sydney Style

Sydneysiders are an optimistic lot. Most Sydney living happens under the sun and the stars: street cafes, alfresco restaurants, moonlight cinemas, beer gardens, parades...

It follows that locals have an almost pathological disdain for overdressing. As the innumerable supermodel-spangled billboards around town attest, less is more in the Sydney fashion stakes, and showing some skin is de rigueur. And if you've got a hot bod, why not decorate it? Full-sleeve tattoos have become mainstream, while hospitality workers sans piercings are rare. Smoking is as popular as ever – will future Sydney echo with an emphysemic death rattle?

Ultimately, Sydney's relentlessly chipper attitude tends to bowl over (or at least distract from) any obstacle. A swim in the surf, a bucket of prawns by the harbour, a kickin' DJ set or a multicultural meal goes a long way towards convincing the majority of residents that life here is pretty darn good.

Top Tip

Partying in the Cross

Traditionally Sydney's premier party precinct, Kings Cross has stacks of bars ranging from snug locals to superslick posing palaces to raucous booze barns. However, it's been hard-hit by the central Sydney licensing laws introduced in 2014 resulting in 1.30am lockouts and a ban on alcohol service after 3am. Many of the late-night clubs are soldiering on regardless, but some of the heat has moved elsewhere. On the upside, the streets look less like a war zone in the wee hours and certainly feel safer.

deliciously inventive dishes drawing inspiration from all over Asia. Plates are designed to be shared, although waiters can arrange half serves for solo diners. (☏02-9380 6744; www.chinadoll.com.au; 4/6 Cowper Wharf Rdwy; mains $34-46; ⏱noon-2.30pm & 6pm-late; ☒Kings Cross)

Piccolo Bar
CAFE $

11 ☒ Map p124, C4

A surviving slice of the old bohemian Cross, this tiny cafe hasn't changed much in over 60 years. The walls are covered in movie-star memorabilia, and Vittorio Bianchi still serves up strong coffee, omelettes and abrasive charm, as he's done for over 40 years. (www.piccolobar.com.au; 6 Roslyn St; mains $6-16; ⏱8am-4pm; ☎; ☒Kings Cross)

Zinc
CAFE $

12 ☒ Map p124, C3

Zinc was built on breakfasts, which remain excellent. But so are the tasty sandwiches and salads offered at lunchtime. The good-looking staff are full of smiles. (☏02-9358 6777; 77 Macleay St; breakfast $9-14, lunch $9-19; ⏱7am-4pm; ✐; ☒Kings Cross)

Drinking

Kings Cross Hotel
PUB, CLUB

13 Map p124, B5

With five floors above ground and one below, this grand old pub is a hive of boozy entertainment which positively swarms on weekends. Head up to the roof bar for awesome city views, or drop by the 2nd-floor band room for a blast of live music. (www.kingscrosshotel.com.au; 244-248 William St; ⏱noon-1am Sun-Thu, to 3am Fri & Sat; ☒Kings Cross)

Sugarmill
BAR

14 🍺 Map p124, B4

For a bloated, late-night, Kings Cross bar, Sugarmill is actually pretty cool. Columns and high pressed-tin ceilings hint at its banking past, while the band posters plastered everywhere do their best to dispel any lingering capitalist vibes. Ten-dollar meals and drag queen–hosted bingo pull in the locals. For barbecue with a view, head to **Sweethearts** (www.sweetheartsbbq.com.au) on the rooftop. (www.sugarmill.com.au; 33 Darlinghurst Rd; ⏱10am-5am; ☒Kings Cross)

World Bar

BAR, CLUB

15 Map p124, B5

World Bar (a reformed bordello) is an unpretentious grungy club with three floors to lure in the backpackers and cheap drinks to loosen things up. DJs play indie, hip hop, power pop and house nightly. There are live bands on Fridays, but Wednesday (The Wall) and Saturday (Cakes) are the big nights. (☏02-9357 7700; www.theworldbar.com; 24 Bayswater Rd; ⏱3pm-3am; ☒Kings Cross)

Kit & Kaboodle

CLUB

The club above Sugarmill (see **14** Map p124, B4) comes into its own on a Sunday night, when hospitality workers take advantage of the cheap drinks to kick-start their belated weekend. (www.kitkaboodle.com.au; 33 Darlinghurst Rd; ⏱8pm-late Thu-Sun; ☒Kings Cross)

Soho

BAR, CLUB

16 Map p124, B4

Housed in the art deco Piccadilly Hotel, Soho is a dark, sexy establishment with smooth leather lounges that have felt the weight of Keanu Reeves', Nicole Kidman's and Ewan McGregor's celebrity booties; it's rumoured to be where Kylie Minogue met Michael Hutchence. The downstairs club hosts regular events. (www.sohobar.com.au; 171 Victoria St; ⏱10am-midnight Mon-Wed, to 4am Thu & Sun, to 6am Fri & Sat; ☒Kings Cross)

Understand
Rugby League

There's plenty to yell about if you arrive during the winter footy season. In Australia, 'footy' can mean a number of things – including Australian Football League (aka Aussie rules), rugby union and soccer – but in Sydney's it's usually rugby league.

Rugby league is king in NSW, and Sydney is considered one of the world capitals for the code. The pinnacle of the game is widely held to be the annual State of Origin where NSW battles Queensland. This best-of-three series even overshadows test matches, such as the annual Anzac Test between Australia's Kangaroos and New Zealand's Kiwis.

The National Rugby League comp runs from March to October, climaxing in the sell-out grand final at ANZ Stadium. You can catch games every weekend during the season, played at the home grounds of Sydney's various tribes. The easiest ground to access is the 45,500-seat Sydney Football Stadium (aka Allianz Stadium), home of the Sydney Roosters. Other Sydney-based teams include Russell Crowe's beloved South Sydney Rabbitohs, Wests Tigers, Parramatta Eels and the Manly-Warringah Sea Eagles.

Understand

Sydney's Music Scene

Rock & Alternative

In the 1970s and '80s Australia churned out a swag of iconic pub rockers, with Sydney bands INXS and Midnight Oil at the forefront. During the '90s and noughties, when guitar bands came back into vogue, contrary Sydney popped a pill and headed to the disco. Most of the significant Australian acts of the era formed elsewhere, with the exception of garage rockers the Vines, cartoon punks Frenzal Rhomb, singer-songwriter Alex Lloyd and jangly sentimentalists the Whitlams. In the meantime, Sydney's most successful musical export was children's novelty act the Wiggles.

Things have been looking up in recent years, with the city turning out the likes of electro popsters the Presets, hard rockers Wolfmother, folky siblings Angus & Julia Stone, alternative rock lads Boy & Bear, indie reggae kids Sticky Fingers and indie disco kids the Jezabels.

Pop & Dance

Australia loves its pop stars and dance divas, and is currently churning them out at a rate of knots in reality TV shows. Others have taken the more traditional route to pop stardom: starring in a cheesy soap opera. Melbourne can lay claim to Kylie Minogue, but Sydney makes do with Delta Goodrem and Natalie Imbruglia. Then there's homegrown boyband 5 Seconds of Summer, who hit number one in 11 countries in 2014 with their self-titled debut album.

Sydney loves to cut a rug, and you'll find a bit of everything being played around the dance clubs, from drum and bass to electro. Homegrown dance music is made by the likes of RÜFÜS, Flume, Flight Facilities, Bag Raiders and Art vs Science, and spun by popular DJs such as Timmy Trumpet, Tigerlily, Alison Wonderland and J-Trick.

Opera

With an opera house as its very symbol, no discussion of Sydney's musical legacy is complete without mentioning Dame Joan Sutherland (1926–2010), the Eastern Beaches lass who became one of the greatest opera singers of the 20th century. Her legacy can be seen in the success of Opera Australia and singers such as Cheryl Barker.

Bootleg BAR

17 🚇 Map p124, B4

If you're looking for a quieter, more sophisticated alternative to the Darlinghurst Rd melee (or just a chance to catch your breath), slink into a booth at this bar-cum-Italian eatery and order a wine from the list. The decor's a strange mix of industrial chic and Chicago lounge bar, but it works. (www.bootlegbar. com.au; 175 Victoria St; ⏰5-11pm Sun, Tue & Wed, to 1am Thu-Sat; 🚇Kings Cross)

Jimmy Lik's COCKTAIL BAR

18 🚇 Map p124, B4

Understated, slim and subtle, Jimmy's is very cool, with benches almost as long as the Southeast Asian–influenced cocktail list (try a Mekong Mary with vodka, tomato juice and chilli *nahm jim*). (📞02-8354 1400; www.jimmyliks.com; 188 Victoria St; ⏰5-11pm Mon-Thu, noon-midnight Fri-Sun; 🚇Kings Cross)

Tilbury PUB

19 🚇 Map p124, A3

Once the dank domain of burly sailors and salty ne'er-do-wells, the Tilbury now sparkles. Yuppies, yachties, suits, gays and straights alike populate the light, bright interiors. The restaurant, bar and gin garden are particularly popular on lazy Sunday afternoons. And sailors can still get a beer! (📞02-9368 1955; www.tilburyhotel.com.au; 12-18 Nicholson St; ⏰11am-11pm; 🚇Kings Cross)

Entertainment

El Rocco JAZZ, COMEDY

20 ⭐ Map p124, B5

Between 1955 and 1969 this was the city's premier finger-snappin', beret-wearing boho cellar bar, hosting performances by Frank Sinatra and Sarah Vaughan. Those heady days are long gone but live jazz is back on the agenda, along with the Happy Endings Comedy Club (www.happyendingscomedyclub. com.au) on Saturdays. (www.elrocco.com. au; 154 Brougham St; ⏰5pm-midnight Mon-Sat, 5-10pm Sun; 🚇Kings Cross)

Old Fitz Theatre THEATRE

21 ⭐ Map p124, A4

Is it a pub? A theatre? A bistro? Actually, it's all three. Grassroots company Red Line Productions stages loads of new Australian plays here. (www.oldfitz theatre.com; 129 Dowling St; 🚇Kings Cross)

Explore

Bondi to Coogee

Improbably good-looking arcs of sand framed by jagged cliffs, the Eastern Beaches are a big part of the Sydney experience. Most famous of all is the broad sweep of Bondi Beach, where the distracting scenery and constant procession of beautiful bods never fail to take your mind off whatever it was you were just thinking about...

The Sights in a Day

☀ Grab your swimming gear and head to the beach. Catch the bus to **Bondi** (p134) and spend some time strolling about and soaking it all in. If the weather's right, stop for a swim. Once you're done, take the clifftop path to **Tamarama Beach** (p138) and on to **Bronte Beach** (p138). Take a slight detour up to Bronte's excellent **Three Blue Ducks** (p140) for lunch.

☀ Continue on the coastal path through **Waverley Cemetery** (p138), **Clovelly Beach** (p139) and on to **Coogee Beach** (p139). Board a bus back to wherever you're staying and freshen up for the night ahead.

☾ Have a beer on the terrace of the **North Bondi RSL** (p143) as the sun goes down and then head clear across the beach to **Icebergs Dining Room** (p141) for dinner with a view. Pop over to **Anchor** (p143) for a frosty margarita and then continue on to **Neighbourhood** (p142) for a nightcap.

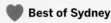

Top Sights
Bondi Beach (p134)

Best of Sydney

Eating
Three Blue Ducks (p140)

Icebergs Dining Room (p141)

A Tavola (p141)

Beaches
Bondi Beach (p134)

Bronte Beach (p138)

Clovelly Beach (p139)

Tamarama Beach (p138)

Markets
Bondi Markets (p145)

Getting There

🚆 **Train** The Eastern Suburbs line heads to Bondi Junction, which is 2.5km from Bondi Beach.

🚌 **Bus** For Bondi catch bus 333 (express), 380, 381, 382 or 389. For Bronte take bus 378. For Clovelly take bus 339 or 360. For Coogee take bus 373 via Oxford St, bus 372 via Surry Hills, or bus 313, 314 or 353 from Bondi Junction.

Top Sights
Bondi Beach

Definitively Sydney, Bondi is one of the world's great beaches: ocean and land collide, the Pacific arrives in great foaming swells and all people are equal, as democratic as sand. It is the closest ocean beach to the city centre (8km away), has consistently good (though crowded) waves, and is great for a rough-and-tumble swim. If the sea's angry or you have small children in tow, try the saltwater sea baths at either end of the beach.

Map p136, D2

Campbell Pde

380

Don't Miss

Bondi Pavilion

Built in the Mediterranean Georgian Revival style in 1929, **Bondi Pavilion** (www.waverley.nsw.gov.au; Queen Elizabeth Dr; admission free; ⏰9am-5pm; 🚌380) is more cultural centre than changing shed, although it does have changing rooms, showers and lockers. It has a free art gallery upstairs, a theatre out the back and various cafes and a bar lining the ocean frontage.

Surf Lessons

North Bondi is a great beach for learning to surf. **Let's Go Surfing** (📞02-9365 1800; www.letsgosurfing. com.au; 128 Ramsgate Ave; board & wetsuit hire 1hr/2hr/ day/week $25/30/50/150; ⏰9am-5pm), down the far northern end of the beach, caters to practically everyone, with classes for grommets (ages seven to 16; 1½ hours $49) and adults (two hours $99). And if you just want to hire gear to hit the waves, you can do that too.

Dry Land Activities

Prefer wheels to fins? There's a skate ramp at the beach's southern end. If posing in your budgie smugglers (speedos) isn't having enough impact, there's an outdoor workout area near the North Bondi Surf Club. Coincidentally (or perhaps not), this is the part of the beach where the gay guys hang out.

Bondi Icebergs

With supreme views of Bondi Beach, **Bondi Icebergs Swimming Club** (📞02-9130 4804; www. icebergs.com.au; 1 Notts Ave; adult/child $6/4; ⏰6.30am-6.30pm Fri-Wed) is a fair dinkum Sydney institution. Only hardened winter-swimming fanatics can become fully fledged members, but anyone can pay for a casual entry.

☑ Top Tips

▶ The two surf clubs – Bondi and North Bondi – patrol the beach between sets of red and yellow flags, positioned to avoid the worst rips and holes. Thousands of unfortunates have to be rescued from the surf each year (enough to make a TV series about it), so don't become a statistic – swim between the flags.

▶ At the beach's northern end there's a grassy spot with coin-operated barbecues.

▶ Surfers carve up sandbar breaks at either end of the beach.

✕ Take a Break

Soak up the views from the **Crabbe Hole** (Map p136, D3; Lower Level, 1 Notts Ave; mains $10-12; ⏰7am-5pm; 🚌380) cafe.

Booze is banned on the beach, so head up to the North Bondi RSL (p143) for a cooling beer on the terrace.

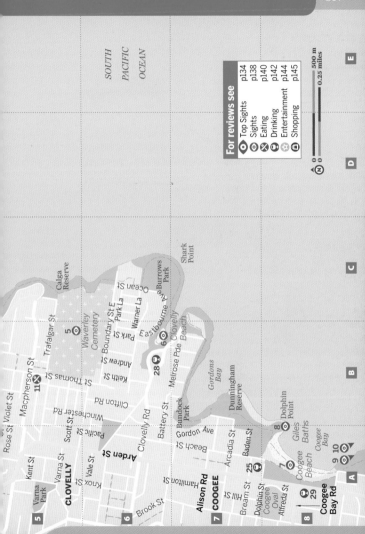

SOUTH
PACIFIC
OCEAN

For reviews see

◉ Top Sights	p134
◯ Sights	p138
✕ Eating	p140
◯ Drinking	p142
◯ Entertainment	p144
◯ Shopping	p145

0   500 m
0   0.25 miles

Shark
Point

Calga
Reserve

Ocean St

Burrows
Park

Waverley
Cemetery

Park La

Warner La

Boundary St E

Eastbourne Ave

Melrose Pde Clovelly

Trafalgar St

Macpherson St

St Thomas St

Andrew St

Keith St

Clovelly Rd

Gordons
Bay

Rose St

Violet St

Kent St

Varna St

Varna
Park

CLOVELLY

Knox St

Vale St

Winchester Rd

Scott St

Pacific Rd

Clifton Rd

Arden St

Battery St

Burdock
Park

Gordon Ave

Dunningham
Reserve

Dolphin
Point

Giles
Baths

Coogee
Bay

Beach St

Arcadia St

COOGEE

Alison Rd

Hamilton St

Bream St

Hill St

Dolphin St

Coogee
Oval

Alfreda St

Coogee
Beach

Coogee
Bay Rd

Brook St

5 ◉
11 ✕
28 ◯
6 ◉
25 ◯
29 ◯
7 ◉
8 ◉
9 ◉
10 ◉

Sights

Aboriginal Rock Engravings
ARCHAEOLOGICAL SITE

1 ◉ Map p136, E1

On the clifftop fairways of Bondi Golf & Diggers Club, a short walk north from Bondi Beach, lies a flat patch of rock carved by the Eora Aboriginal people (look for it about 20m south-east of the enormous chimney, and watch out for flying golf balls). Some of the images are hard to distinguish, though you should be able to make out marine life and the figure of a man. The carvings were regrooved in the 1960s to help preserve them. (5 Military Rd; ☐380)

Ben Buckler Point
VIEWPOINT

2 ◉ Map p136, E2

Forming the northern tip of the Bondi horseshoe, this point offers wonderful views of the entire beach. The 235-tonne, car-sized rock near the beach's northern tip was spat out of the sea during a storm in 1912. The lookout is at the end of Ramsgate Ave, or you can follow the trail which runs along the rocks from the beach. (Ramsgate Ave; ☐380)

Tamarama Beach
BEACH

3 ◉ Map p136, C4

Surrounded by high cliffs, Tamarama has a deep tongue of sand with just 80m of shoreline. Diminutive, yes, but ever-present rips make Tamarama the most dangerous patrolled beach in New South Wales; it's often closed to swimmers. It's hard to picture now, but between 1887 and 1911 a roller coaster looped out over the water as part of an amusement park. (Pacific Ave; ☐361)

Bronte Beach
BEACH

4 ◉ Map p136, C4

A winning family-oriented beach hemmed in by sandstone cliffs and a grassy park, Bronte lays claims to the title of the oldest surf lifesaving club in the world (1903). Contrary to popular belief, the beach is named after Lord Nelson, who doubled as the Duke of Bronte (a place in Sicily), and not the famous literary sorority. There's a kiosk and a changing room attached to the surf club, and covered picnic tables near the public barbecues. (Bronte Rd; ☐378)

Waverley Cemetery
CEMETERY

5 ◉ Map p136, B5

Many Sydneysiders would die for these views...and that's the only way they're going to get them. Blanketing the clifftops between Bronte and Coogee, the white marble gravestones here are dazzling in the sunlight. Eighty thousand people have been interred here since 1877, including writer Henry Lawson and cricketer Victor Trumper. It's an engrossing (and surprisingly uncreepy) place to explore, and maybe to spot a whale offshore during winter. (www1.waverley.nsw.gov.au/cemetery; St Thomas St; ⊙7am-6pm; ☐378)

MANFRED GOTTSCHALK / GETTY IMAGES ©

Bronte and Tamarama beaches

Clovelly Beach
BEACH

6 Map p136, B6

It might seem odd, but this concrete-edged ocean channel is a great place to swim, sunbathe and snorkel. It's safe for the kids, and despite the swell surging into the inlet, underwater visibility is great. A beloved friendly grouper fish lived here for many years until he was speared by a tourist. Bring your goggles, but don't go killing anything...On the other side of the car park is the entrance to the Gordons Bay Underwater Nature Trail, a 500m underwater chain guiding divers past reefs, sand flats and kelp forests. (Clovelly Rd; 339)

Coogee Beach
BEACH

7 Map p136, A8

Bondi without the glitz and the posers, Coogee (locals pronounce the double *o* as in the word 'took') has a deep sweep of sand, historic ocean baths and plenty of green space for barbecues and frisbee hurling. Between the world wars, Coogee had an English-style pier, with a 1400-seat theatre and a 600-seat ballroom...until the surf took it. (Arden St; 372-373)

Giles Baths
SWIMMING

8 Map p136, A8

If you've got kids, shark-paranoia, or surf isn't your thing, don't worry; Sydney's blessed with a string of 40 ocean

Understand
Surf Lifesaving

Surf lifesaving originated in Sydney, although red-and-yellow-capped volunteer lifesavers have since assumed iconic status across Australia. Despite the macho image, many lifesavers are women, and a contingent of gay and lesbian lifesavers march in the Sydney Mardi Gras Parade.

At summer surf carnivals all along the coast you can see these dedicated athletes wedge their speedos up their butt cracks and launch their surf boats (butt cheeks grip the seats better than speedos, apparently). Ask a local surf lifesaving club for dates, or contact Surf Life Saving Australia for info.

pools up and down the coast, most of them free. At Coogee Beach's northern end, below Dolphin Point, Giles Baths is what's known as a 'bogey hole' – a semiformal rock pool open to the surging surf. (admission free; ☐372-373)

Wylie's Baths SWIMMING

9 Map p136, A8

On the rocky coast south of Coogee Beach, this superb seawater pool (1907) is targeted at swimmers more than splashabouts. After your swim, take a yoga class ($18), enjoy a massage, or have a coffee at the kiosk, which has magnificent ocean views. (☏02-9665 2838; www.wylies.com.au; 4B Neptune St; adult/child $4.80/1; ⏱7am-7pm Oct-Mar, to 5pm Apr-Sep; ☐372-374)

McIvers Baths SWIMMING

10 Map p136, A8

Perched against the cliffs south of Coogee Beach and well-screened from passers-by, McIvers Baths has been

popular for women's bathing since before 1876. Its strict women-only policy has made it popular with an unlikely coalition of nuns, Muslim women and lesbians. Small children of either gender are permitted. (Beach St; admission 20c; ☐372-374)

Eating

Three Blue Ducks CAFE $$

11 Map p136, B5

These ducks are a fair waddle from the water, but that doesn't stop queues forming outside the graffiti-covered walls for weekend breakfasts. The adventurous chefs have a strong commitment to using local, organic and fair-trade food whenever possible. (☏02-9389 0010; www.threeblueducks.com; 141-143 Macpherson St; breakfast $16-25, lunch $24-31, dinner $28-32; ⏱7am-2.30pm Sun-Tue, 7am-2.30pm & 6-11pm Wed-Sat; ☐378)

Icebergs Dining Room

ITALIAN $$$

12 Map p136, D3

Poised above the famous Icebergs swimming pool, Icebergs' views sweep across the Bondi Beach arc to the sea. Inside, bow-tied waiters deliver fresh, sustainably sourced seafood and steaks cooked with elan. To limit the hip-pocket impact, call in at lunchtime for a pasta and salad. (☎02-9365 9000; www.idrb.com; 1 Notts Ave; mains $40-48; ⏱noon-3pm & 6.30-11pm Tue-Sun; 🚌380)

Lox, Stock & Barrel

DINER, DELI $$

13 Map p136, C1

Stare down the barrel of a smoking hot bagel and ask yourself one question: Wagyu corned beef Reuben, or homemade pastrami and Russian coleslaw? In the evening the menu sets its sights on steak, lamb shoulder and slow-roasted eggplant. (☎02-9300 0368; www.loxstockandbarrel.com.au; 140 Glenayr Ave; breakfast & lunch $11-18, dinner $29; ⏱7am-3.30pm daily, 6pm-late Wed-Sun)

A Tavola

ITALIAN $$

14 Map p136, C1

Carrying on the tradition of its Darlinghurst sister, Bondi's A Tavola gathers around a big communal marble table where, before the doors open, the pasta-making action happens. Expect robust flavours, sexy waiters and delicious homemade pasta. (☎02-9130 1246; www.atavola.com.au; 75 Hall St; mains $22-38; ⏱noon-3pm Wed-Sun, 5.30-11pm daily)

The Shop

CAFE $

15 Map p136, C1

Operating as both a cafe and a wine bar (with a name that reflects neither), this tiny space serves cooked breakfasts, pastries, sandwiches, salads and, in the evening, tapas and burgers. It's a bit self-consciously cool, but the food and coffee are excellent. (www.theshopbondi.com; 78 Curlewis St; mains $10-18; ⏱6am-10pm; 🚌389)

Bondi Trattoria

ITALIAN $$

16 Map p136, C2

For a Bondi brunch, you can't go past the trusty 'Trat', as it's known in these parts. Tables spill out onto Campbell Pde for those hungry for beach views, while inside there's a trad trat feel: wooden tables, and the obligatory Tuscan mural

---

✅ Top Tip

Bondi Junction Interchange

Bondi Junction, 2.5km from Bondi Beach and 6km from Circular Quay, is the transport hub for the Eastern Beaches. The Eastern Suburbs train line terminates beneath the main bus station, right next to the Westfield shopping mall. Although buses head straight to the beaches from the city, it's usually much quicker to catch a train to Bondi Junction and then head upstairs to connect by bus to the beach.

and black-and-white photography. As the day progresses, pizza, pasta and risotto dominate the menu. (📞02-9365 4303; www.bonditrattoria.com.au; 34 Campbell Pde; breakfast $9-19, lunch $17-29, dinner $19-36; ⏱8am-late; 🚌380)

Pompei's ITALIAN $$

17 Map p136, D2

The pizza here is among the best in Sydney, but it's the northern Italian dishes whipped up by expat Giorgio Pompei that are really special. Try the handmade ravioli stuffed with spinach, ricotta and nutmeg, and leave some space for a scoop of their legendary gelato. (📞02-9365 1233; www.pompeis.com.au; 126-130 Roscoe St; mains $21-34; ⏱noon-11pm Tue-Fri, 8.30am-11pm Sat & Sun; 🚌389, 380, 333)

Sabbaba MIDDLE EASTERN $

18 Map p136, C2

There are more boardshorts than black coats on view at this Middle Eastern joint in Bondi's main Hassidic strip. Falafels served in pitta are a quick-fire bargain, and there's a sticky-sweet array of baklava to finish off with. There are branches in Westfield Sydney and Newtown. (📞02-9365 7500; www.sabbaba.com.au; 82 Hall St; mains $9-17; ⏱11am-10pm; 🥦; 🚌389)

Jed's Foodstore CAFE $

19 Map p136, C1

Jed's is so relaxed, you'll feel like you're back in a uni share house. Reggae

mellows the tattooed staff, who sing and groove around; dudes sip coffee outside as kids and dogs run amok. Grab a seat for the Caribbean-style jerked potato scramble and a strong coffee. (📞02-9365 0022; 60 Warners Ave; mains $9-19; ⏱6.30am-3.30pm Mon-Fri, to 4.40pm Sat & Sun; 🚌389)

Sean's Panaroma AUSTRALIAN $$$

20 Map p136, E1

Sean Moran's ever-changing menu is chalked on a blackboard in this modest little dining room. Come for the ocean views, hearty seasonal dishes and friendly service, but beware the $5 per person surcharge on weekends. (📞02-9365 4924; www.seanspanaroma.com.au; 270 Campbell Pde; mains $39-45; ⏱6-11pm Wed-Fri, noon-11pm Sat & Sun; 🚌380)

Drinking

Neighbourhood BAR

21 Map p136, C1

The natural habitat for the curious species known as the Bondi Hipster, this smart food and wine bar has a brick-lined interior giving way to a wood-lined courtyard. Bondi Radio broadcasts live from a booth near the kitchen. (www.neighbourhoodbondi.com.au; 143 Curlewis St; ⏱5.30-11pm Mon-Thu, noon-11pm Fri, 9am-11pm Sat & Sun; 🚌380-382)

Anchor
BAR

22 🚇 Map p136, C3

Surfers, backpackers and the local cool kids slurp down icy margaritas at this bustling bar at the south end of the strip. It's also a great spot for a late snack. (www.anchorbarbondi.com; 8 Campbell Pde; ⏰4.30pm-midnight Tue-Fri, 12.30pm-midnight Sat & Sun; 🚌380-382)

North Bondi RSL
BAR

23 🚇 Map p136, E2

This Returned and Services League bar ain't fancy, but with views no one can afford and drinks that everyone can, who cares? The kitchen serves good cheap nosh, including a dedicated kids' menu. Bring ID, as nonmembers need to prove that they live at least 5km away. (www.north bondirsl.com.au; 120 Ramsgate Ave; ⏰noon-10pm Mon-Fri, 10am-midnight Sat, 10am-10pm Sun; 🚼; 🚌380-382)

Bucket List
BAR

24 🚇 Map p136, D2

On a sunny day, fight for a seat on the Bucket List's in-demand terrace. Sip on a ice-cold beverage while watching the passing parade or gazing aimlessly out to sea. If the weather turns, there are plenty of brightly decorated nooks inside where you can shelter from the elements. (www.thebucketlistbondi.com; Bondi Pavilion; ⏰11am-midnight; 🚌380)

Coogee Pavilion
BAR

25 🚇 Map p136, A7

With its numerous indoor and outdoor bars, Mediterranean-influenced eatery, kids' play area, giant scrabble set and glorious adults-only rooftop, this vast complex has brought a touch of inner-city glam to Coogee. Built in 1887, the building originally housed an aquarium and swimming pools. (www. merivale.com.au/coogeepavilion; 169 Dolphin St; ⏰7.30am-late; 🚼; 🚌372-374)

Corner House
BAR

26 🚇 Map p136, C3

Three spaces – the Kitchen (wine and pizza bar), Dining Room (restaurant) and Living Room (cocktail bar) – make this a particularly happy house. It's up the hill in Bondi proper so the vibe's more local, attracting an eclectic range of Bondi natives. (www.thecorner house.com.au; 281 Bondi Rd; ⏰5pm-midnight Tue-Sat, 3-10pm Sun; 🚌380-382)

Icebergs Bar
BAR

The neighbouring eatery, Icebergs Dining Room (see 12 🍴 Map p136, D3), is more famous, but the ooh-la-la Icebergs Bar is a brilliant place for a drink. Colourful sofas and ritzy cocktails do little to distract from the killer views looking north across Bondi Beach. Dress sexy and make sure your bank account is up to the strain. (www.idrb.com; 1 Notts Ave; ⏰noon-midnight Tue-Sat, 10am-10pm Sun; 🚌380-382)

Understand
Aboriginal Art

- -

Australian Aboriginal art is one of the oldest forms of creativity in the world, dating back more than 50,000 years. Art has always been integral to Aboriginal life – a connection between the past and the present, the supernatural and the earthly, the people and the land. For the Eora people of the Sydney area, it took the form of engravings on rocky headlands and stencilled handprints in caves.

It inevitably comes as a surprise to stumble across an art form that's so ancient in such a modern city, yet Sydney is built on top of a giant gallery. Until recently not much attention was paid to such things and much was covered over or destroyed. But with the dot paintings from distant deserts being celebrated, Sydneysiders have started to wake up to the treasure trove that's literally under their feet.

Beach Road Hotel   PUB

27 Map p136, C1

Weekends at this big boxy pub are a boisterous multilevel alcoholiday, with Bondi types (bronzed, buff and brooding) and woozy out-of-towners playing pool, drinking beer and digging live bands and DJs. (www.beachroadbondi. com.au; 71 Beach Rd; ⊗11am-midnight Mon-Sat, 10am-10pm Sun; 🚇389)

Clovelly Hotel   PUB

28 Map p136, B6

A recently renovated megalith on the hill above Clovelly Beach, this pub has a shady terrace and water views – perfect for postbeach Sunday-afternoon bevvies. Entertainment includes live music, poker comps, quiz nights, happy hours and even a mothers' group. (☏02-9665 1214; www.clovellyhotel. com.au; 381 Clovelly Rd; ⊗10am-midnight Mon-Sat, to 10pm Sun; 🚇339)

Coogee Bay Hotel   PUB, CLUB

29 Map p136, A8

This rambling, rowdy complex packs in the backpackers for live music, open-mic nights, comedy and big-screen sports in the beaut beer garden, sports bar and Selina's nightclub. Sit on a stool at the window overlooking the beach and sip on a cold one. (www.coogeebayhotel.com.au; 253 Coogee Bay Rd; ⊗7am-late; 🚇374)

Entertainment

Bondi Openair Cinema   CINEMA

30 Map p136, D2

Enjoy open-air screenings by the sea, with live bands providing prescreening entertainment. Online bookings recommended. (www.openaircinemas. com.au; Dolphin Lawn, next to Bondi Pavilion; tickets $15-45; ⊗Jan & Feb)

Shopping

Surfection
CLOTHING, ACCESSORIES

31 Map p136, C2

Selling boardies, bikinis, sunnies, shoes, watches, tees… even luggage – Bondi's coolest surf shop has just about everything the stylish surfer's heart might desire (except for spray-in hair bleach; you'll still need to take your paper bag to a discreet chemist for that). Old boards hang from the ceiling, while new boards fill the racks. (www.facebook.com/Surfection; 31 Hall St; ⏰10am-5.30pm; 🚌380-382)

Rip Curl
CLOTHING, ACCESSORIES

32 Map p136, C2

The quintessential Aussie surf shop, Rip Curl began down south in Victoria, but drops in perfectly overlooking the Bondi shore breaks. Beyond huge posters of burly surfer dudes and beach babes, you'll find bikinis, watches, boardshorts, wetsuits, sunglasses, hats, T-shirts and (surprise!) surfboards. (📞02-9130 2660; www.ripcurl.com.au; 82 Campbell Pde; ⏰9am-6pm; 🚌380-382)

Bondi Markets
MARKET

33 Map p136, D1

On Sundays, when the kids are at the beach, their school fills up with Bondi characters rummaging through tie-dyed secondhand clothes, original fashion, books, beads, earrings, aromatherapy oils, candles, old records and more. There's a farmers market here on Saturdays. (www.bondimarkets.com. au; Bondi Beach Public School, Campbell Pde; ⏰9am-1pm Sat, 10am-4pm Sun; 🚌380-382)

Gertrude & Alice
BOOKS

34 Map p136, C2

This shambolic secondhand bookshop and cafe is so un-Bondi: there's not a model or a surfer in sight. Locals, students and academics hang out reading, drinking coffee and acting like Americans in Paris. Join them for some lentil stew and theological discourse around communal tables. (📞02-9130 5155; www.gertrudeandalice.com.au; 46 Hall St; ⏰7.30am-8.30pm; 🚌380-382)

Aquabumps
ARTS

35 Map p136, C1

Photographer/surfer Eugene Tan has been snapping photos of Sydney's sunrises, surf and sand for 15 years. His colourful prints hang in this cool space, just a splash from Bondi Beach. (📞02-9130 7788; www.aquabumps.com; 151 Curlewis St)

Kemenys
WINE

36 Map p136, B2

A short walk up (and then a wobble down) the hill from Bondi Beach, Kemenys occupies a large soft spot in the hearts, minds and livers of Bondi locals. Proffering the best local and imported wines, ales and spirits to the surf set since 1960, it has staunchly resisted being taken over by the big chains. Respect. (📞138 881; www. kemenys.com.au; 137-147 Bondi Rd; ⏰8am-9pm; 🚌380-382)

Local Life
A Day in Watsons Bay

The narrow peninsula ending in South Head is one of Sydney's most sublime spots. The view of the harbour from the Bondi approach, as Old South Head Rd leaves the sheer ocean cliffs to descend to Watsons Bay, is breathtaking. Watsons Bay was once a small fishing village, as evidenced by the tiny heritage cottages that pepper the narrow streets.

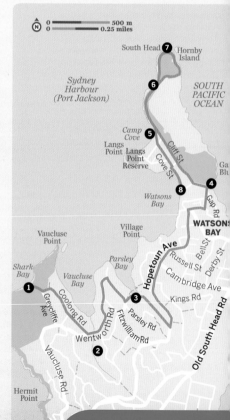

Getting There

⚓ Regular ferries run between Circular Quay and Watsons Bay.

🚌 Routes to Watsons Bay include the 325 via Vaucluse and the 380 via Bondi.

❶ Nielsen Park

Something of a hidden gem, this leafy harbourside park with a sandy beach was once part of the 206-hectare Vaucluse House estate. Visit on a weekday when it's not too busy. The park encloses **Shark Beach** – a great spot for a swim, despite the ominous name – and **Greycliffe House**, an 1851 Gothic sandstone pile (not open to visitors).

❷ Vaucluse House

Vaucluse House (📞02-9388 7922; www. sydneylivingmuseums.com.au; Wentworth Rd; adult/child $8/4; 🕙11am-4pm Fri-Sun; 🚌325) is an imposing, turreted specimen of Gothic Australiana set among 10 hectares of lush gardens. Building commenced in 1805 but the house was tinkered with into the 1860s. Decorated with European period pieces, it offers visitors a rare glimpse into early (albeit privileged) colonial life.

❸ Parsley Bay

A hidden gem, this little **bay** (enter near 80a Hopetoun Ave; 🚌325) has a calm swimming beach, a lawn dotted with sculptures for picnics and play, and a cute suspension bridge. Keep an eye out for water dragons as you walk down through the bush.

❹ The Gap

On the ocean side of Watsons Bay, the Gap is a dramatic clifftop lookout where proposals and suicides happen with similar frequency.

❺ Camp Cove

Immediately north of Watsons Bay, this swimming beach is popular with both families and topless sunbathers. When Governor Phillip realised Botany Bay didn't cut it as a site for a settlement, he sailed north into Sydney Harbour, dropped anchor and sunk his boots into Camp Cove's gorgeous golden sand on 21 January 1788.

❻ Lady Bay

Also known as Lady Jane, this diminutive gay nudist beach sits at the bottom of a cliff, on top of which is a Royal Australian Navy facility. To get here, follow the clifftop walking track from (somewhat aptly named) Camp Cove. All together now: 'In the navy…'

❼ South Head

The **South Head Heritage Trail** passes old battlements and a path heading down to Lady Bay, before continuing on to the candy-striped Hornby Lighthouse and the sandstone Lightkeepers' Cottages (1858) on South Head itself. The harbour views and crashing surf on the ocean side make this a very dramatic and beautiful spot indeed.

❽ Watsons Bay Beach Club

One of the great pleasures in life is languishing in the rowdy beer garden of the **Watsons Bay Hotel** (www.watsonsbayhotel. com.au; 1 Military Rd, Watsons Bay; 🕙10am-midnight Mon-Sat, to 10pm Sun; ⛴Watsons Bay) after a day at the beach. Stay to watch the sun go down over the city and grab some seafood if you're hungry.

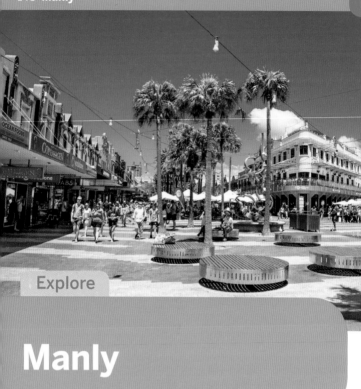

Explore

Manly

Laid-back Manly clings to a narrow isthmus between ocean and harbour beaches abutting North Head, Sydney Harbour's northern gatepost. With its shaggy surfers, dusty labourers and relaxed locals, it makes for a refreshing change from the stuffier harbour suburbs nearby. The surf's good and as the gateway to the Northern Beaches, it makes a popular base for the board-riding brigade.

The Sights in a Day

☀ Jump on the ferry at Circular Quay for the leisurely and extremely beautiful journey to Manly. Before it gets too hot, hire a bike from **Manly Bike Tours** (p153), grab a map at the visitor centre in front of the wharf, and explore **North Head** (p151), dropping into the historic former **Quarantine Station** (p151) on the way back. Return the bikes, cool off with a dip at **Manly Cove** (p152) and head to **Belgrave Cartel** (p154) for lunch.

☀ It'll take less than an hour to breeze around **Manly Art Gallery & Museum** (p153). If you're not planning on visiting Darling Harbour's Sydney Aquarium, **Manly Sea Life Sanctuary** (p153) is a trimmed down alternative – plus you can swim with sharks here. Head along the Corso and spend the rest of the day body-surfing and lazing around **Manly Beach** (p151).

☾ Shuffle into a seat with a view at **Hugos Manly** (p153) on Manly Wharf and tuck into a pizza. Finish up with a drink on the water's edge at **Manly Wharf Hotel** (p155).

 **Best of Sydney**

Eating
Chat Thai (p154)

Beaches
Manly Beach (p151)

Manly Cove (p152)

For Free
Manly Art Gallery & Museum (p153)

Getting There

⚓ **Ferry** Frequent ferry services head directly from Circular Quay, making this by far the best (and most scenic) means to get to Manly. Regular Sydney ferries take 30 minutes while fast ferries take 18 minutes.

🚌 **Bus** Prepay express bus E70 takes 37 minutes to reach Manly Wharf from the city, while regular bus 171 takes about an hour.

South Steyne, Manly Beach

Sights

Manly Beach BEACH

1 ◎ Map p150, C2

Sydney's second most famous beach stretches for nearly two golden kilometres, lined by Norfolk Island pines and scrappy midrise apartment blocks. The southern end of the beach, nearest the Corso, is known as South Steyne, with North Steyne in the centre and Queenscliff at the northern end; each has its own surf lifesaving club. (🚇Manly)

North Head NATIONAL PARK

2 ◎ Map p150, D4

About 3km south of Manly, spectacular, chunky North Head offers dramatic cliffs, lookouts and sweeping views of the ocean, the harbour and the city; hire a bike and go exploring. (North Head Scenic Dr; 🚌135)

Quarantine Station HISTORIC BUILDING

3 ◎ Map p150, D4

From 1835 to 1983 this eerie-but-elegant complex was used to isolate new arrivals suspected of carrying disease, in an attempt to limit the spread of cholera, smallpox and bubonic plague. These days the 'Q Station' has been reborn as a tourist destination with a museum, accommodation, restaurants and a whole swathe of tour options. (☎02-9466 1551; www.quarantinestation.com.au; 1 North Head Scenic Dr; admission free; ☉museum 10am-4pm Sun-Thu, to 8pm Fri & Sat; ☐135)

Shelly Beach

BEACH

4 ◉ Map p150, E3

This sheltered north-facing ocean cove is just a short 1km walk from the busy Manly beach strip. The tranquil waters are a protected haven for marine life, so it offers wonderful snorkelling. (☷Manly)

Fairy Bower Beach

BEACH

5 ◉ Map p150, D3

Indulge your mermaid fantasies (the more seemly ones at least) in this pretty triangular ocean pool set into the rocky shoreline. The life-size sea nymphs of Helen Leete's bronze sculpture *Oceanides* (1997) stand on the edge, washed by the surf. Fairy Bower is best reached by the promenade heading around Manly Beach's southern headland. (Bower Lane; ☐135)

Manly Cove

BEACH

6 ◉ Map p150, B3

Split in two by Manly Wharf, this sheltered enclave has shark nets and calm water, making it a popular choice for

---

Understand
Surfin' Northern Beaches

Sydney's Northern Beaches have been synonymous with surfing ever since the Beach Boys effused about 'Australia's Narrabeen' in *Surfin' USA*. This 20km stretch of coast between Manly and Palm Beach has been described as the most impressive urban surfing landscape in the world. The sun-bronzed locals who swim and catch the waves at Manly, Freshwater, Curl Curl, Dee Why, Collaroy, Narrabeen, Mona Vale, Newport, Bilgola, Avalon, Whale and Palm Beaches are uniformly proud to agree.

Each of these beaches has a markedly different atmosphere. Dee Why is a no-fuss family beach fronted by chunky apartments, some good cafes and ubiquitous surf shops. Its gentler waves are good for beginner surfers. By contrast, Narrabeen is hard-core surf turf. It all comes to an end in long, lovely Palm Beach, famous as the setting for cheesy TV soap *Home & Away*.

For updates on what's breaking where, see www.coastalwatch.com or www.realsurf.com. If you're keen to learn to surf, contact Manly Surf School. If it's gear you're after, try Aloha Surf (p157).

families with toddlers. Despite the busy location, the clear waters have plenty of appeal. (⊜Manly)

Manly Sea Life Sanctuary
AQUARIUM

7 ◎ Map p150, A3

This ain't the place to come if you're on your way to Manly Beach for a surf. Underwater glass tubes enable you to become alarmingly intimate with 3m grey nurse sharks. Reckon they're not hungry? **Shark Dive Xtreme** (introductory/certified dives $280/205) enables you to enter their world. (☏1800 199 742; www.manlysealifesanctuary. com.au; West Esplanade; adult/child $25/15; ⏰9.30am-5pm; ⊜Manly)

Manly Art Gallery & Museum
MUSEUM

8 ◎ Map p150, A3

A short stroll from Manly Wharf, this passionately managed community gallery maintains a local focus, with exhibits of surfcraft, camp swimwear and beachy bits and pieces. There's also a ceramics gallery, and lots of old Manly photos to peer at. (www.manly. nsw.gov.au; West Esplanade; admission free; ⏰10am-5pm Tue-Sun; ⊜Manly)

Manly Surf School
SURFING

9 ◎ Map p150, C1

Offers two-hour surf lessons year-round (adult/child $70/55), as well as private tuition. Also runs surf safaris up to the Northern Beaches, including two

⬤ Local Life
Manly-Warringah Sea Eagles

The local rugby league team are neighbourhood heroes, having won the premiership twice in the past decade. Home games are played further north at Brookvale, but Manly's pubs are lively places to watch matches. The local pub scene revolves around the Corso and Manly Wharf.

lessons, lunch, gear and city pick-ups ($120). (☏02-9932 7000; www.manlysurf school.com; North Steyne Surf Club; ⊜Manly)

Manly Bike Tours
CYCLING

10 ◎ Map p150, B3

Hires bikes and runs daily two-hour bike tours around Manly (10.30am, $89, bookings essential). (☏02-8005 7368; www.manlybiketours.com.au; 54 West Promenade; hire per hr/day from $15/31; ⏰9am-6pm; ⊜Manly)

Eating

Hugos Manly
ITALIAN $$

11 ✕ Map p150, B3

Occupying an altogether more glamorous location than its Kings Cross parent, Hugos Manly serves the same acclaimed pizzas but tops them with harbour views and an expanded Italian menu. A dedicated crew concocts cocktails, or you can just slide in for

Local Life
The Corso

At the heart of the 'hood is the Corso, a part-pedestrian mall leading from the Manly ferry terminal to Manly's ocean beach. If you're looking for a surf shop, newsagency, bookshop, pharmacy, ATM, laundromat, liquor store, pub, pie shop or kebab counter, you'll find it here. The mood is suburban and relaxed, with local kids splashing around in the fountains and spaced-out surfies shuffling back to the ferry after a hard day carving up the swell.

a cold beer. (✆02-8116 8555; www.hugos.com.au; Manly Wharf; pizzas $20-28, mains $32-38; ⏱noon-midnight; 🚢Manly)

Barefoot Coffee Traders   CAFE $

13 🍴 Map p150, B2

Run by surfer lads serving fair-trade organic coffee from a bathroom-sized shop, Barefoot heralds a new wave of Manly cool. Food is limited but the Belgian chocolate waffles go magically well with a macchiato. (18 Whistler St; items $3-6; ⏱6.30am-5.30pm; 🚢Manly)

Chat Thai   THAI $

Set inside Manly Wharf, this branch of the **Thaitown favourite** (✆02-9211 1808; www.chatthai.com.au; 20 Campbell St; mains $10-20; ⏱10am-2am; 🚇Central) misses out on the harbour views but delivers on flavour. It's located beside Hugos Manly (see 11 🍴 Map p150, B3). (✆02-9976

2939; www.chatthai.com.au; Manly Wharf; mains $10-18; ⏱11am-9.30pm; 🚢Manly)

Belgrave Cartel   CAFE $$

13 🍴 Map p150, B2

Little Cartel may be grungy but it's nowhere near as sinister as it sounds; the only drugs being peddled here are pure, unadulterated caffeine and utterly addictive Italian-influenced fare (antipasti, salads, pulled pork sliders, pasta). 'Mismatched everything' seems to be the design brief. (✆02-9976 6548; www.cartelgroup.co; 6 Belgrave St; small plates $6-18, mains $16-26; ⏱7am-10pm Sun, 6am-2pm Mon & Tue, to midnight Wed-Sat; 🚢Manly)

Pure Wholefoods   VEGETARIAN $

14 🍴 Map p150, B3

This wholefood minimart has a great little street cafe serving organic vegetarian goodies, including flavoursome flans, salads, nori rolls, cakes, cookies, wraps, burgers and smoothies. Vegan, raw-food, sugar-free, gluten-free and dairy-free purists are also catered for. (✆02-8966 9377; www.facebook.com/PureWholefoods; 10 Darley Rd; mains $10-15; ⏱7am-5pm; 🍴; 🚢Manly)

BenBry Burgers   BURGERS $

15 🍴 Map p150, B2

A popular takeaway assembling juicy gourmet burgers for beach bums and backpackers. (www.benbryburgersmanly.com; 5 Sydney Rd; burgers $6.50-14; ⏱11am-9pm; 🍴; 🚢Manly)

Manly Wharf Hotel

Bower Restaurant

MODERN AUSTRALIAN **$$**

 16 Map p150, D3

Follow the foreshore east from Manly's ocean beach to this salty little cafe/restaurant, within spray's breath of the sea. There's lots of seafood on the menu and the sandy surfer-gal staff aren't afraid to let Olivia Newton-John wail on the stereo. (☏02-9977 5451; www.thebowerrestaurant.com.au; 7 Marine Pde; breakfast $14-19, lunch $22-30; ⊙8am-5pm; ☒Manly)

Drinking

Manly Wharf Hotel

PUB

17 Map p150, B3

Harking back to 1950s design (bamboo and stone feature walls etc), this water-front pub is perfect for sunny afternoon beers. Tuck away a few schooners after a hard day in the surf, then pour yourself onto the ferry. Sports games draw a crowd and DJs liven up Sunday afternoons. There's good pub food, too, with specials throughout the week. (www.manlywharfhotel.com.au; Manly Wharf; ⊙11.30am-midnight; ☒Manly)

Understand

Sydney Cinema

Since Fox Studios opened in Moore Park in 1998, Sydney has starred in various blockbusters such as the *Matrix* trilogy, *Mission Impossible 2* and *X-Men Origins: Wolverine*. Sydneysider Baz Luhrmann's *Moulin Rouge, Australia* and *The Great Gatsby* were made here, as were numerous other films set everywhere from Antarctica *(Happy Feet II)* to a galaxy far, far away (the *Star Wars* prequels).

Yet more emblematic of the soul of Sydney cinema is the decidedly low budget **Tropfest** (www.tropfest.com), where thousands of locals shake out their blankets in Centennial Park in December to watch entries in the largest short-film festival in the world.

Beginnings

One of the most successful early Australian films was *The Sentimental Bloke* (1919), which included scenes filmed in Manly, the Royal Botanic Garden and Woolloomooloo. Government intervention in the form of both state and federal subsidies reshaped the future of the country's film industry through the 1970s. Sydneysiders who benefitted from the subsequent renaissance in the industry included Oscar-nominated director Peter Weir (who made such films as *Gallipoli, Dead Poets Society, The Truman Show* and *Master and Commander*) and Oscar winners Mel Gibson and Nicole Kidman.

Boom & Beyond

The 1990s saw films that cemented Australia's reputation as a producer of quirky comedies about local misfits: *Strictly Ballroom* (with locations in Pyrmont and Marrickville), *Muriel's Wedding* (Parramatta, Darlinghurst and Darling Point) and *The Adventures of Priscilla, Queen of the Desert* (Erskineville). Australian actors who got their cinematic start around this time include Hugo Weaving, David Wenham, New Zealand–born Russell Crowe, Cate Blanchett, Heath Ledger and Toni Collette.

The new millennium got off to a good start with the likes of *Lantana* and *Finding Nemo*, but since then it's fair to say that Sydney has failed to set big screens alight.

The Corso (p154)

Hotel Steyne
PUB

18 Map p150, C2

Boasting numerous bars over two levels, this landmark pub accommodates everyone from sporty bogans to clubby kids to families. The internal courtyard isn't flash (people still smoke here!), but the rooftop bar more than makes up for it with wicked views over the beach. Live bands and DJs entertain. (☎02-9977 4977; www.steynehotel.com.au; 75 The Corso; ⏰9am-3am Mon-Sat, to midnight Sun; 🚢Manly)

Bavarian Bier Café
BEER HALL

19 Map p150, B3

Transplanted from **York Street** (☎02-8297 4111; www.bavarianbiercafe.com; 24 York St; ⏰11am-midnight; 🚇Wynyard) to the beach, the Bavarian offers 10 brews on taps and 10 more imported beers by the bottle. (www.bavarianbiercafe.com; Manly Wharf; ⏰11am-midnight Mon-Fri, 9am-midnight Sat & Sun; 🚢Manly)

Shopping
Aloha Surf
SPORTS, CLOTHING

20 Map p150, B1

Longboards, shortboards, bodyboards, skateboards and surfing fashion. (☎02-9977 3777; www.alohasurfmanly.com.au; 42 Pittwater Rd; ⏰9am-6pm; 🚢Manly)

The Best of
Sydney

Sydney's Best Walks

Sydney's Best...

Interior dome of the Queen Victoria Building (p65)
ANDREW WATSON / GETTY IMAGES ©

Best Walks
The City's Green Corridor

🏃 The Walk

There's no better introduction to Sydney's top sights than this stroll through the corridor of parkland that runs through the heart of Sydney, ending in the organised chaos of Circular Quay. The route can be marched in an hour, or stretched out to the best part of a day, with extended stops along the way.

Start Anzac Memorial; 🚇 Museum

Finish Circular Quay; 🚈 Circular Quay

Length 5km; two hours

✗ Take a Break

There are cafes and restaurants in the Art Gallery and Royal Botanic Garden, or you could hold on until Circular Quay for a ritzy meal at **Aria** (p36) or a cheaper bite at **Sailors Thai Canteen** (p36).

Hyde Park (p51)

CHRISTINE WEHRMEIER / GETTY IMAGES ©

❶ Anzac Memorial

Start at the **Anzac Memorial** (p55), a striking art deco structure that commemorates the soldiers of the Australian and New Zealand Army Corps (Anzacs) who served in WWI. The pines planted nearby grew from seeds gathered at Gallipoli in Turkey, the site of the Anzacs' most renowned WWI campaign.

❷ Hyde Park

Leave the memorial by the northern door and head straight through the centre of **Hyde Park** (p51), past the **Pool of Remembrance**. Hyde Park is split in two by Park St; cross over and continue through the avenue of trees to the **Archibald Memorial Fountain**.

❸ The Domain

Veer right at the fountain, cross towards the ornate **Lands Department Building** and enter the Domain. Sculptures dot the park, including a reclining Henry Moore figure, and Brett Whiteley's *Almost Once* (1991) – two giant matches, one burnt – rising from the ground near the **Art Gallery of NSW** (p48).

❹ Mrs Macquaries Point

The Domain ends in spectacular fashion at **Mrs Macquaries Point** (p27), where a vista of the harbour, Fort Denison, Opera House, Harbour Bridge and city skyline suddenly appears. Clouds of sulphur-crested cockatoos disturb the peace with their raucous caws during the day; at night it's a romantic spot for an after-dinner stroll.

❺ Royal Botanic Garden

Follow the swoop of Farm Cove into the beautiful surrounds of the **Royal Botanic Garden** (p26). Keep an eye out for **Government House** as you pass beneath it.

❻ Sydney Opera House

As you exit through Queen Elizabeth II Gate the heaven-sent sails of the **Sydney Opera House** (p24) are directly in front of you. Clamber

up to their base and circumnavigate Bennelong Point to enjoy it from every angle.

❼ Sydney Writers Walk

A series of metal discs cast into the Circular Quay promenade hold ruminations from prominent Australian writers (and the odd literary visitor).

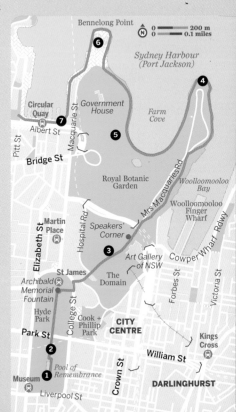

Best Walks
Bondi to Coogee

🏃 The Walk

Arguably Sydney's most famous, most popular and best walk, this coastal path shouldn't be missed. Both ends are well connected to bus routes, as are most points in between should you feel too hot and bothered to continue – although a cooling dip at any of the beaches en route should cure that (pack your swimmers). There's little shade on this track, so make sure you dive into a tub of sunscreen before setting out.

Start Bondi Beach; 🚌 380

Finish Coogee Beach; 🚌 372, 373

Length 6km; three hours

🍴 Take a Break

The best lunch option is Bronte's **Three Blue Ducks** (p140). To get there, cut through the reserve immediately before Waverley Cemetery and head up Macpherson St.

❶ Bondi Beach

Starting at **Bondi Beach** (p134), take the stairs up the south end to Notts Ave, passing above the glistening Bondi Icebergs pool complex. Step onto the clifftop trail at the end of Notts Ave. Walking south, the blustery sandstone cliffs and grinding Pacific Ocean couldn't be more spectacular (watch for dolphins, whales and surfers).

❷ Tamarama Beach

Small but perfectly formed **Tamarama Beach** (p138) has a deep reach of sand, totally disproportionate to its width.

❸ Bronte Beach

Descend from the clifftops onto **Bronte Beach** (p138) and take a dip, lay out a picnic under the Norfolk Island pines or head to a cafe for a snack and a caffeine hit. After your break, pick up the path at the other end of the beach.

OLIVER STREWE / GETTY IMAGES ©

Coastal walk from Bondi (p134) to Coogee (p139)

4 Waverley Cemetery

Some famous Australians are among the subterranean denizens of the amazing cliff-edge **Waverley Cemetery** (p138). On a clear day this is a prime vantage point for whale watchers.

5 Clovelly Beach

Pass the locals enjoying a beer or a game of lawn balls at the **Clovelly Bowling Club**, then breeze past the cockatoos and canoodling lovers in **Burrows Park** to sheltered **Clovelly Beach** (p139), a fave with families.

6 Gordons Bay

Follow the footpath up through the car park, along Cliffbrook Pde, then down the steps to the upturned dinghies lining Gordons Bay, one of Sydney's best shore-dive spots.

7 Dolphin Point

This grassy tract at Coogee Beach's northern end has superb ocean views and the **Giles Baths** (p139) ocean pool. A sobering shrine commemorates the 2002 Bali bombings. Coogee was hit hard by the tragedy, with 20 of the 89 Australians killed coming from hereabouts. Six members of the Coogee Dolphins rugby league team died in the blast.

8 Coogee Beach

The trail then lands you smack-bang onto glorious **Coogee Beach** (p139). Swagger up to the rooftop of the **Coogee Pavilion** (p143) and toast your efforts with a cold beverage.

Best Walks
Manly Scenic Walkway

🏃 The Walk

This epic walk traces the coast west from Manly past million-dollar harbour-view properties and then through a rugged 2.5km section of Sydney Harbour National Park that remains much as it was when the First Fleet sailed in. Make sure you carry plenty of water, slop on some sunscreen, slap on a hat and wear sturdy shoes.

Start Manly Cove; 🚢 Manly

Finish Spit Bridge; 🚌 176–180 (to city), 140–144 (to Manly)

Length 9km; four hours

🍴 Take a Break

There aren't any eateries en route, so fortify yourself at **Hugos Manly** (p153) beforehand or stock up for a picnic at **Pure Wholefoods** (p154).

❶ Manly Cove

Pick up a walk brochure (which includes a detailed map) from the **Hello Manly** (p190) visitor information centre by Manly Wharf. Walk along **Manly Cove** (p152) and pick up the path near **Manly Sea Life Sanctuary** (p153).

❷ Fairlight Beach

After 700m you'll reach Fairlight Beach, where you can scan the view through the heads. Yachts tug at their moorings as you trace the North Harbour inlet for the next 2km.

❸ Forty Baskets Beach

Forty Baskets Beach sits at the point where the well-heeled streets of Balgowlah Heights end and bushclad Sydney Harbour National Park commences. The picnic area is cut off at high tide.

❹ Reef Beach

Kookaburras cackle as you enter the national park and approach Reef Beach. Despite what you might have heard,

Manly Scenic Walkway

LEONARDO PATRIZI / GETTY IMAGES ©

this little cove is neither nude nor full of dudes; the Manly Council put paid to that in 1993. Now it's often deserted.

5 Dobroyd Head

The track becomes steep, sandy and rocky further into the park – keep an eye out for wildflowers, spiders in bottlebrush trees and fat goannas sunning themselves. The views from Dobroyd Head are unforgettable. Check out the deserted 1930s sea shacks at the base of Crater Cove cliff.

6 Grotto Point

Look for **Aboriginal rock carvings** on an unsigned ledge left of the track before the turn-off to **Grotto Point Lighthouse**. Rugged and beautiful, **Washaway Beach** is a secluded little spot on the point's eastern edge.

7 Clontarf Beach

Becalmed **Castle Rock Beach** is at the western end of the national park. From here the path winds around the rear of houses to **Clontarf Beach**, a low-lapping elbow of sand facing the Spit Bridge that's popular with families, with grassy picnic areas.

8 Spit Bridge

Sandy Bay follows and then Fisher Bay before you reach Spit Bridge, a bascule bridge that connects Manly to Mosman and opens periodically to let boats through to Middle Harbour.

Best
Beaches

KEVIN OSBORNE / FOX FOTOS / GETTY IMAGES ©

Whether you join the procession of the bronzed and the beautiful at Bondi, or surreptitiously slink into a deserted nook hidden within Sydney Harbour National Park, the beach is an essential part of the Sydney experience. Even in winter, watching the rollers break while you're strolling along the sand is exhilarating.

Best Harbour Beaches

Shark Beach The pick of the harbour beaches, hidden within leafy Nielsen Park. (p147)

Camp Cove Family-friendly, with golden sand and gentle swells. (p147)

Lady Bay Discreetly tucked under South Head, this is the best of the nude beaches. (p147)

Parsley Bay A well-kept secret, concealed behind the mansions of Vaucluse. (p147)

Manly Cove Shark nets and clear, calm waters, right by the ferry wharf. (p152)

Best Ocean Beaches

Bondi Beach Australia's most famous beach, for good reason. (p134)

Clovelly Beach Despite the concrete, this is a magical swimming and snorkelling spot. (p139)

Bronte Beach Perfect for bucket-and-spade family days and picnic lunches. (p138)

Manly Beach Learn to surf or simply laze upon the 2km of golden sand. (p151)

Tamarama Beach Treacherous waves pound this pretty scoop of sand. (p138)

Top Tips

▶ Always swim between the red and yellow flags on lifesaver-patrolled beaches. Not only are these areas patrolled, they're positioned away from dangerous rips and holes.

▶ Due to pollution from stormwater drains, avoid swimming in the ocean for one day and in the harbour for three days after heavy rains.

Best
Historic Buildings

Best Homes

Vaucluse House William Wentworth's Vaucluse mansion is a rare surviving colonial harbourside estate. (p147)

Elizabeth Bay House Another harbourside home, built in a gracious Georgian style in the heart of Lizzie Bay. (p125)

Susannah Place Giving the people who lived in slum houses their rightful place in history. (p32)

Government House A fittingly grand residence for the governors of NSW since 1837. (p27)

Best Religious Buildings

St Mary's Cathedral Beamed in from Gothic Europe, the grand Catholic cathedral is awash with colour when the sun hits the stained glass. (p54)

Great Synagogue A mismatch of architectural styles, maybe, but a beautiful one. (p56)

St James' Church Francis Greenway's elegant, understated church is perhaps his crowning achievement. (p56)

St Andrew's Cathedral Based on York Minster, the city's Anglican cathedral stakes its place in Sydney society next to the Town Hall. (p57)

Sze Yup Temple A surprising find on the edge of Glebe, this small Chinese temple is perpetually wreathed in incense. (p87)

Best Administrative Buildings

Town Hall The Victorians may have seemed buttoned up, but not when it came to their buildings, as the exuberant Town Hall attests. (p57)

Hyde Park Barracks Convict architect Francis Greenway's beautiful prison, housing a fascinating museum. (p54)

Victoria Barracks Still used by the military, these Georgian army barracks can be visited

KIMBERLEY COOLE / GETTY IMAGES ©

on free guided tours. (p119)

Customs House An elegant Victorian building put to new use. (p32)

Best Commercial Buildings

Queen Victoria Building The most unrestrained and ornate survivor of the Victorian era. (p65)

Martin Place A stretch of grand bank buildings and the High Victorian former General Post Office, the most iconic building of its time. (p51)

Best
Eating

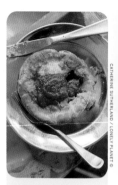

Sydney's cuisine rivals that of any world city. Melbourne makes a big deal of its Mediterranean melting pot, but Sydney truly celebrates Australia's place on the Pacific Rim, marrying the freshest local ingredients with the flavours of Asia, the Americas and, of course, its colonial past.

Where to Eat

Sydney's top restaurants are properly pricey, but eating out needn't be expensive. There are plenty of ethnic eateries where you can grab a cheap pizza or a zingy bowl of noodles. Cafes are a good bet for a solid, sometimes adventurous and usually reasonably priced meal.

Advance Australian Fare

Australia is blessed with first-rate produce from farms and fisheries across the nation. The tropical north provides pineapples, mangoes and even winter strawberries, while cooler southern climes lend themselves to fine wines and cheeses. These come together in a fresh, flavoursome, multicultural collision on dining tables across Sydney.

Wine & BYO

Most licensed restaurants have a respectable wine list and there's almost always at least a handful of wines sold by the glass. Sydney is blessed with enlightened licensing laws that allow you to BYO (bring your own) wine and sometimes beer to restaurants with a BYO licence. You'll usually be charged a corkage fee (even if your bottle's got a screw cap) at either a per-person or per-bottle rate, but it's generally cheaper than choosing off the wine list.

☑ Top Tips

▶ Tipping isn't compulsory in Australia, but if the service is passable most folks tip 10% (particularly at better restaurants). If anything gets your goat, you don't have to tip at all. Tipping isn't expected at cafes, but there's often a jar where customers can sling loose change.

Best Modern Australian

Quay Inventive fine dining with the best views in Sydney. (p35)

Rockpool Celebrity chef Neil Perry's flagship is one of Sydney's very best eateries. (p57)

Icebergs Dining Room (p141)

Best Italian

Icebergs Dining Room Seafood and steaks by the seashore. (p141)

A Tavola Homemade pasta dishes packed with big tastes. (p141)

Best Thai

Longrain Delicious modern Thai concoctions and piquant cocktails. (p109)

Chat Thai Reasonably priced, loaded with flavour and constantly buzzing. (p154)

Best Chinese

Mr Wong Cantonese dishes served to the smart set in a louche warehouse basement. (p57)

Spice Temple An atmospheric underground den dealing in intense flavours. (p58)

Best Japanese

Tetsuya's Book months ahead for this groundbreaking restaurant's Japanese-French degustation. (p57)

Cho Cho San Japanese elegance celebrated in both the decor and the cuisine. (p126)

Best South American

Porteño Delicious slowcooked meat and bucketloads of atmosphere. (p108)

Bodega Latin-influenced tapas, loud music and a festive vibe. (p109)

Best Cafes

Three Blue Ducks Serves the sort of creative cafe fare that Sydney excels in. (p162)

Single Origin Roasters Serious caffeine fiends serving tasty bites, too. (p110)

Best Bakeries

Bourke Street Bakery Neighbourhood legend serving delectable pastries, both sweet and savoury. (p109)

Adriano Zumbo The macaron man spreads joy in multiple Sydney locations. (p77)

Best
Green Spaces

Despite its urban sprawl, Sydney is a surprisingly green metropolis. National parks ring the city and penetrate right into its heart. Large chunks of the harbour are still edged with bush, while parks cut their way through the skyscrapers and suburbs.

ANDREW WATSON / GETTY IMAGES ©

Best Gardens

Royal Botanic Garden
Well-tended lawns, interesting botanical collections and ever-present harbour views make this Sydney's most beautiful park. (p26)

Chinese Garden of Friendship A traditional arrangement of streams, ponds and paths to soothe the city's stresses. (p73)

Best Formal Parks

Hyde Park A shady avenue of trees, lit with fairy lights at night, makes this an inviting place for a stroll. (p51)

Victoria Park At the foot of the university, its formal paths are popular with more than just students. (p83)

Best Open Expanses

The Domain The extensive lawns are used for large-scale public gatherings. (p50)

Centennial Park Formal bits, wild bits and a whir of joggers, cyclists and horse riders circling the central avenues. (p119)

Jubilee & Bicentennial Parks Interlinked grassy expanses lining the harbour in Glebe. (p88)

Best with Kids

Tumbalong Park An urban park with an engaging adventure playground. (p75)

Nielsen Park A tucked-away, leafy harbourside park with a blissful shark-netted beach. (p147)

☑ Top Tips

▶ In summer you can watch a movie under the stars at Mrs Macquaries Point, Centennial Park and the lawn facing Bondi Beach.

Best Views

Mrs Macquaries Point Jutting out into the harbour, offering the best views of the city skyline. (p27)

Observatory Hill Trudge up from the Rocks to this grassy knoll and gaze over Walsh Bay. (p32)

Best
With Kids

With boundless natural attractions, a climate favouring outdoor activities and an inbuilt inclination towards being laid-back, Sydney is a top spot to bring the kids. In summer there are plenty of beaches to keep everyone happy, and when it rains, there are many indoor institutions geared to the junior tourist.

Family & Children's Tickets

Most sights, entertainment venues and transport providers offer a discount of up to 50% off the full adult rate for children, although the upper age limit can vary widely (anything from 12 to 18 years of age). Many places also let under-fives or under-threes in for free. Family tickets are common at big attractions, generally covering two adults and two children.

Beaches

The calm waters of Sydney's harbour beaches are great for kids. If you're paranoid about sharks, head to the netted areas at Shark Beach or Manly Cove. Most of Sydney's surf beaches have free saltwater pools.

Best Attractions for Kids

Powerhouse Museum
Hands-on experiments, big chunks of machinery and an interactive Wiggles exhibition. (p86)

Art Gallery of NSW
The Gallery Kids program includes free shows and tailored discovery trails. (p48)

Sydney Opera House
Offers Kids in the House performances, including Babies Proms. (p24)

Sydney Sea Life Aquarium Fill in a few hours finding Nemo, sea dragons, disco-lit jellyfish, dugongs, and gargantuan rays and sharks. (p70)

L'ALTRA FIGURA, 1984, GIULIO PAOLINI / ANDREW WATSON / GETTY IMAGES ©

☑ **Top Tips**

▶ Scan kiddie shops for copies of *Sydney's Child,* a free magazine listing activities and businesses catering to anklebiters, or check the online family-events calendar at www.webchild.com.au.

▶ For an extra cost, car-hire companies will supply and fit child safety seats (compulsory for children under seven).

Monkey Baa Theatre Company Fun-filled productions designed for the youngest culture vultures. (p79)

Best
Bars & Pubs

In a city where rum was once the currency, it's little wonder that drinking plays a big part in the social scene – whether it's knocking back some tinnies at the beach, schmoozing after work, or warming up for a night on the town. Sydney offers plenty of choice in drinking establishments, from the flashy to the trashy.

WAYNE FOGDEN / GETTY IMAGES ©

The Sydney Scene

Sydneysiders are generally gregarious and welcoming of visitors, and the easiest place to meet them is at the pub. Most inner-city suburbs have retained their historic corner pubs – an appealing facet of British life the colonists were loath to leave behind. The addition of beer gardens has been an obvious improvement, as has the banning of smoking from all substantially enclosed licensed premises.

The cheapest places to drink in are Returned and Services League (RSL) clubs. In a tourist-friendly irony, locals are barred unless they're members, but visitors who live more than 5km away are welcome (you'll need to bring proof).

Lockouts & Last Drinks

In an effort to cut down on alcohol-fuelled violence, tough new licensing laws have been introduced to a large area of the central city bounded by the Rocks, Circular Quay, Woolloomooloo, Kings Cross, Darlinghurst, Haymarket and the eastern shores of Darling Harbour.

Within this zone, licensed venues are not permitted to admit people after 1.30am. However, if you arrive before then, the venue is permitted to continue serving you alcohol until 3am.

☑ Top Tips

▶ Traditional Sydney pubs serve middies (285mL) and schooners (425mL), while pints (570mL) are the domain of Anglo-Celtic theme pubs. Australian pubs abandoned pints long ago because beer would go warm in the summer heat before you'd finished your glass.

Opera Bar (p37)

Best Bars

Baxter Inn Whiskies by the dozen in a back-alley hideaway. (p60)

Wild Rover A modern-day speakeasy disguised as an abandoned clothing warehouse. (p110)

Pocket Alternative music, hip decor, comfy couches and table service. (p111)

Best Pubs

Hero of Waterloo Historic pub with live music and its own dungeon. (p38)

Courthouse Hotel Back-street pub with a beer garden and a wonderfully relaxed vibe. (p92)

Best for Beer

Local Taphouse Dozens of craft beers to work your way through. (p111)

Lord Nelson Brewery Hotel Arguably Sydney's oldest pub but inarguably an excellent micro-brewery. (p37)

Best Wine Bars

The Winery The greenest spot for a cheeky tipple, right in the heart of Surry Hills. (p112)

121BC Gather around the communal table for fine wine and free-flowing bonhomie. (p113)

Best Cocktails

Hinky Dinks Happy Days are here again in this 1950s-themed cocktail bar. (p111)

Grandma's Kooky in the extreme, with tiki cocktails to boot. (p60)

Best Views

O Bar Revolve around the 47th floor of the Australia Square tower. (p62)

Blu Bar on 36 Head up to the top of the Shangri-La for a bird's-eye view over the bridge. (p39)

Best Outdoors

Beresford Hotel Join the beautiful people in Sydney's swishest beer garden. (p113)

Opera Bar Opera House, Harbour Bridge, Circular Quay – all present and visible. (p37)

Best
Gay & Lesbian

DAVID HILL / GETTY IMAGES ©

Gays and lesbians have migrated to Oz's Emerald City from all over Australia, New Zealand and the world, adding to a community that is visible, vibrant and an integral part of the city's social fabric. Locals will assure you that things aren't as exciting as they once were, but Sydney is still indisputably one of the world's great queer cities.

Social Acceptance

These days few Sydneysiders bat an eyelid at same-sex couples holding hands on the street, but the battle for acceptance has been long and protracted. Sydney is now relatively safe, but it still pays to keep your wits about you, particularly at night.

Party Time

Mardi Gras (www.mardigras.org.au) is the city's main gay pride festival. **Harbour City Bears** (www.harbourcitybears.com.au) runs Bear Pride in August, while **Leather Pride Week** (www.sydneyleatherpride.org) is a moveable feast but is usually held in winter.

Other regular parties include **Daywash** (www.daywash.com.au), Sydney's most popular daytime party, and **Fag Tag** (www.facebook.com/welovefagtag), organised takeovers of straight bars.

Best Gay Venues

Imperial Hotel The home of Priscilla. (p92)

Palms on Oxford Goodtime, trashy, campy dance venue. (p122)

Best Lesbian Nights

Birdcage Wednesday night takeover of Zanzibar's 2nd floor. (p92)

 Top Tips

▶ NSW's gays and lesbians enjoy legal protection from discrimination and vilification, and an equal age of consent.

▶ Free gay and lesbian rags include the *Star Observer* (www.starobserver.com.au), *SX* (www.gaynewsnetwork.com.au) and *LOTL* (www.lotl.com).

Best
For Free

In Sydney, many of the very best things in life really are free – especially in summer, when lazing around in the sun is one of the city's priceless pleasures.

JAZZDOG / SHUTTERSTOCK ©

Beaches

This ain't the Mediterranean. There are no tightly arranged lines of deckchairs awaiting your paying pleasure at Sydney beaches. Lazing on the beach is part of the Australian birthright and one that's freely available to anyone who cares to roll out a towel. Many of the beaches have ocean pools carved out of the rocks on their headlands and almost all of those are free as well. And if you forget to bring sunblock, ask the surf lifesavers. Chances are they'll give you some. For free. In between patrolling the beach. Also for free.

☑ **Top Tips**

▶ Jump on bus 555 for a free loop around the inner city.

Best Free Galleries

Art Gallery of NSW Free admission, free tours and free Sunday performances for kids. (p48)

Museum of Contemporary Art Special exhibitions are charged but most rooms are free. (p32)

White Rabbit A private collection of contemporary Chinese art, generously displayed for free. (p86)

Best Free Museums

Nicholson Museum Free access to a fascinating collection of antiquities. (p83)

Rocks Discovery Museum Provides an excellent (and completely free) introduction to Australia's oldest neighbourhood. (p32)

Manly Art Gallery & Museum Small museum devoted to local history. (p153)

Best Venues for Free Classical Music

St James' Church Free Wednesday concerts between March and December. (p56)

St Andrew's Cathedral Free organ recitals and concert band performances. (p57)

Town Hall Free organ recitals are held periodically. (p57)

Best
Performing Arts

OLIVER STREWE / GETTY IMAGES ©

Take Sydney at face value and it's tempting to unfairly stereotype its good citizens as a tad shallow, with a tendency towards narcissism. But take a closer look: the arts scene is thriving, sophisticated and progressive – it's not a complete accident that Sydney's definitive icon is an opera house.

Theatre

Probably the most stimulating genre to explore during your visit is theatre. Sydney doesn't have a dedicated theatre district, but that doesn't mean that theatre lovers miss out. The city offers a vigorous calendar of productions from musicals to experimental theatre at venues across the inner city.

Opera

Despite its relatively small population, Australia has produced some of the world's most ear-catching opera singers, including Dames Nellie Melba and Joan Sutherland. The Opera House may be the adored symbol of Sydney, but supporting such a cost-heavy art form is a difficult prospect. New and more obscure works are staged, but it's the big opera hits that put bums on seats.

Classical Music

Sydneysiders live with their stereotype as sun-soaked sports fanatics, but there's still a passionate audience for classical music here (it just barracks a little more quietly). Without having the extensive, highbrow repertoires of European cities, Sydney offers plenty of inspired classical performances – offering the perfect excuse to check out the interior of those famous harbourside sails.

☑ Top Tips

▶ For performance listings, check out Friday's *Shortlist* section of the *Sydney Morning Herald* (www.smh.com.au).

▶ Also check *Time Out* (www.au.timeout.com/sydney) and Sydney events websites www.whatsonsydney.com and http://whatson.cityofsydney.nsw.gov.au.

Dance

Australian dancers have a fearless reputation for awesome physical displays (and sometimes a lack of costume). Performances range from straight-down-the-line traditional ballet with tutus to edgy physical theatre.

State Theatre (p64)

Best Venues

Sydney Opera House
Don't miss the chance to see the House in action. (p24)

State Theatre We don't care what's on, visiting this beautiful place is a joy. (p64)

City Recital Hall The city's premier classical-music venue. (p64)

Metro Theatre The best place to watch touring bands. (p63)

Best Theatre Companies

Sydney Theatre Company The biggest name in local theatre. (p39)

Belvoir Consistently excellent productions in an intimate setting. (p114)

Griffin Theatre Company Based at SBW Stables Theatre; nurtures new Australian writers. (p114)

Best Dance Companies

Sydney Dance Company Australia's top contemporary dance troupe. (p40)

Bangarra Dance Theatre The nation's top Aboriginal performing artists. (p40)

Australian Ballet Regularly brings tutus and bulging tights to the Sydney Opera House. (p40)

Performance Space Edgy works staged within the cavernous sur-rounds of Carriageworks. (p94)

Best
Shopping

MICHAEL TAYLOR / GETTY IMAGES ©

Brash, hedonistic Sydney has elevated shopping to a universal panacea. Feeling good? Let's go shopping. Feeling bad? Let's go shopping. Credit-card bills getting you down? Let's go shopping... Many locals treat shopping as a recreational activity rather than a necessity, evidenced by the teeming cash-flapping masses in Pitt Street Mall every weekend.

What to Buy

Sydney has a thriving fashion scene, and a summer dress or a pair of speedos won't take up much luggage space. Ask at the counters of CD stores or bookshops about what's hot from local bands and authors, or grab a Sydney-set DVD.

For international travellers wanting something quintessentially Australian to take home, head to the Rocks and dig up some opals, an Akubra hat, a Driza-Bone coat or some Blundstone boots. Aboriginal art has soared to global popularity during recent decades. Hunter Valley wine makes a great gift.

Best Shopping Centres

Strand Arcade
Fashion retail at its finest. (p65)

Queen Victoria Building Regal surroundings add a sense of gravitas to any splurge. (p65)

Westfield Sydney
Bafflingly large complex incorporating top restaurants and two prestigious department stores. (p65)

Best Bookshops

Better Read than Dead
An interesting and eclectic range, making for great browsing. (p95)

☑ **Top Tips**

▶ By law, all sales taxes are included in the advertised price.

▶ Apart from the 10% goods and services tax (GST), the only other sales duties payable are on naughty things such as alcohol and tobacco, which are best bought at the duty-free shops at the airport.

Gleebooks A serious book lover's nirvana, with a healthy roster of launches and author talks. (p95)

Best
Markets

Sydney markets make for an interesting excursion. Even if you don't buy anything, the food, the buskers and the people-watching are usually worth the trip. Some markets are very touristy, but others have a distinct local vibe. They run the gamut from groovy to snooty.

Best Local Markets

Bondi Markets Great people-watching and an interesting mix of goods. (p145)

Surry Hills Markets Very much a local affair, but only held monthly. (p117)

Best for Food

Eveleigh Farmers' Market The city's top foodie market, with top-quality snacks and fancy produce. (p88)

The Rocks Markets On Fridays there are less tacky souvenirs and more tasty nosh. (p41)

Fitzroy Gardens This Kings Cross park has an organic food market on Saturday mornings. (p125)

Best for Quality Goods

Paddington Markets Brave the crowds to hunt out good-quality art and craft. (p119)

Best for Cheap Stuff

Paddy's Markets Forget high fashion, head here for bargains and bustle. (p67)

Glebe Markets A more hippyish vibe; good for secondhand clothes. (p95)

Best
Tours

Best Bus Tours

City Sightseeing
(✆02-9567 8400; www.city-sightseeing.com; 24/48hr ticket $40/60; ⏱every 15-45 min, 8.30am-7.30pm) Double-decker buses on two interlinking, 90-minute, hop-on/hop-off loops around Sydney.

Real Sydney Tours
(✆0402 049 426; www.realsydneytours.com.au; 1-3 passengers from $465, additional passengers from $135) Private minibus tours around Sydney or to further-flung locations such as the Blue Mountains and the Hunter Valley.

Best Motorbike Tours

Bikescape
(✆02-9569 4111; www.bikescape.com.au; cnr Parramatta Rd & Young St, Annandale; tours from $195; ☒Stanmore) Harley Davidson city tours and road trips.

Best Cycling Tours

Bike Buffs
(✆0414 960 332; www.bikebuffs.com.au; adult/child $95/70; ☒Circular Quay) Offers four-hour, two-wheeled tours around the harbourside sights, including jaunts over the Harbour Bridge.

Bonza Bike Tours
(✆02-9247 8800; www.bonzabiketours.com; 30 Harrington St; adult/child $119/99; ☒Circular Quay) These bike boffins run a 2½-hour Sydney Highlights tour (adult/child $66/79) and a four-hour Sydney Classic tour ($119/99). Other tours tackle the Harbour Bridge and Manly.

Best Walking Tours

I'm Free
(✆0405 515 654; www.imfree.com.au; 483 George St; admission free; ⏱10.30am, 2.30pm & 6pm; ☒Town Hall) Departing thrice daily from the square between the Town Hall and Cathedral (no bookings taken – just show up), these highly rated three-hour tours are nominally free but are run by guides for tips. The route takes in the Rocks, Circular Quay,

RICHARD CUMMINS / GETTY IMAGES ©

Martin Place, Pitt St and Hyde Park.

Peek Tours
(✆0420 244 756; www.peektours.com.au; ☒Circular Quay) If you find that a cool beverage makes local history easier to digest, this crew will lead you on a two-hour tour of the Rocks, stopping in historic pubs ($60, including a drink at each). It also offers a 90-minute walking tour of Bondi Beach ($40).

The Rocks Walking Tours
(✆02-9247 6678; www.rockswalkingtours.com.au; cnr Argyle & Harrington Sts; adult/child/family $25/12/62; ⏱10.30am & 1.30pm; ☒Circular Quay) Regular 90-minute tours through the historic Rocks, with plenty of not-so-tall tales and interesting minutiae.

Survival Guide

Survival Guide

Before You Go

When to Go

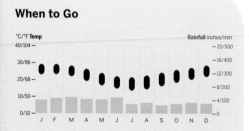

°C/°F Temp
Rainfall inches/mm

→ **Spring (Sep–Nov)**
Sydney's most pleasant
weather: warm and dry
but not too hot. Sea
water still chilly.

→ **Summer (Dec–Feb)**
Long, hot beach days.
Peak season is from
Christmas to the end of
January.

→ **Autumn (Mar–May)**
Sydney's wettest
months, but not cold
until May. Mardi Gras fills
hotels in early March.

→ **Winter (Jun–Aug)**
Cold, short days. Film
festivals, arts festivals
and footy.

Book Your Stay

☑ **Top Tip** Book well in
advance to secure your
top choice of accommoda-
tion and take advantage of
cheaper rates.

→ Sydney is not a cheap
city to stay in.

→ All but the smallest
hotels vary their prices
from day to day depend-
ing on the season, special
events and occupancy.

→ Views play a big part in
determining room prices.

→ Fridays and Saturdays
tend to be more expensive
in all but the most business-
focused hotels, while
Sundays are cheapest.

Useful Websites

Youth Hostel Association
(www.yha.com.au) Hostel
rooms.

Wotif (www.wotif.com) Bookings, including 'mystery
deals'.

Trip Advisor (www.tripadvisor.com) Unvetted, user-generated ratings for a wide range of accommodation.

Lonely Planet (www.lonelyplanet.com/sydney) Traveller forum and listings.

Best Budget

Sydney Harbour YHA (www.yha.com.au) Million-dollar harbour views on a youth-hostel budget.

Cockatoo Island (www.cockatooisland.gov.au) Island camping in the heart of the city.

Bounce (www.bouncehotel.com.au) Boutique budget lodgings with a barbecue on the roof terrace.

Railway Square YHA (www.yha.com.au) An industrial renovation has turned a former Central station parcel shed into a hip hostel.

Wake Up! (www.wakeup.com.au) Flashpackers sleep soundly in this converted 1900 department store.

Blue Parrot (www.blueparrot.com.au) No private rooms, just dorms, and a lazy courtyard strung with hammocks.

Best Midrange

1888 Hotel (www.1888hotel.com.au) A stylish gem in a heritage-listed wool store.

Dive Hotel (www.divehotel.com.au) Contemporary rooms right across from Coogee Beach.

Tara (www.taraguesthouse.com.au) Suburban B&B riding high on charm.

Medusa (www.medusa.com.au) Small colour-saturated suites with large beds, mod-con bathrooms and regal furnishings.

Sydney Harbour Bed & Breakfast (www.bbsydneyharbour.com.au) Hundred-year-old guesthouse with the Rocks and the city on its doorstep.

Adina Apartment Hotel Sydney (www.adinahotels.com.au) Slick, spacious apartments in Sydney's main eating precinct.

Best Top End

QT Sydney (www.qtsydney.com.au) Fun, sexy and completely OTT, this ultra-theatrical hotel is located in the historic State Theatre.

ADGE Boutique Apartment Hotel (www.adgehotel.com.au) Charmingly idiosyncratic and extremely comfortable two-bedroom serviced apartments.

Park Hyatt (www.sydney.park.hyatt.com) There's no better location for Sydney razzle-dazzle.

Simpsons of Potts Point (www.simpsonshotel.com) An oasis of boutique luxury within cooee of gritty Kings Cross.

Westin Sydney (www.westinsydney.com) Choose between heritage rooms with high ceilings, and modern tower rooms.

Pullman Quay Grand Sydney Harbour (www.pullmanhotels.com) These well-designed contemporary apartments place you in the glitzy heart of Sydney.

Arriving in Sydney

☑ **Top Tip** For the best way to get to your accommodation, see p17.

Sydney Airport

➡ The vast majority of visitors to Sydney arrive at **Sydney Airport** (☏02-9667 9111; www. sydneyairport.com.au; Airport Dr, Mascot), 10km south of the city centre.

➡ Taxi fares to the city centre are approximately $45 to $55.

➡ Airport shuttles head to hotels and hostels in the city centre, and some reach surrounding suburbs and beach destinations. Operators include **Sydney Airporter** (☏02-9666 9988; www. kst.com.au; adult/child $15/10), **Super Shuttle** (SSS; ☏1300 018 460; www. signaturelimousinessydney. com.au), **Airport Shuttle North** (☏1300 505 100; www.airportshuttlenorth. com; to Manly 1/2/3 people $41/51/61) and **Manly Express** (☏02-8068 8473; www.manlyexpress.com. au; to Manly 1/2/3 people $43/58/68).

➡ **Airport Link** (www. airportlink.com.au; adult/ child $18/14; ⏰4.30am-12.30am) runs trains from both the domestic and international terminals, connecting into the main train network. They're frequent (every 10 minutes), easy to use and quick (13 minutes to Central), but airport tickets are charged at a hefty premium.

➡ There's a direct bus to Bondi Junction ($4.50, 1¼ hours), which departs roughly every 20 minutes.

Getting Around

Sydneysiders love to complain about their public transport system, but visitors should find it easy to navigate. The train system is the lynchpin, with lines radiating out from Central station.

Train

☑ **Best for...** Getting to Circular Quay, the city centre, Newtown, Surry Hills, Darlinghurst, Kings Cross and Bondi Junction.

➡ **Sydney Trains** (☏131 500; www.sydneytrains.info)

has a large suburban railway web with relatively frequent services.

➡ Trains run from around 5am to 1am.

➡ A short inner-city one-way trip costs $4.

➡ If you don't have an Opal card, purchase your ticket in advance from an automated machine or a counter at the bigger stations.

Bus

☑ **Best for...** Short journeys, and all the places the train doesn't go, especially the Eastern Beaches.

➡ **Sydney Buses** (☏131 500; www.sydneybuses.info) has an extensive network, operating from around 5am to midnight when less frequent NightRide services commence.

➡ You can buy a ticket from the driver on most services ($2.40 to $4.70, depending on the length of the journey), but you'll need an Opal card or prepaid paper ticket (available at newsagents, convenience stores and supermarkets) for prepay-only services.

➡ Prepaid tickets need to be dunked into the green ticket machines as you enter the bus. If you'll be catching buses a lot (but not trains or ferries), consider a prepaid 10-ride TravelTen ticket (sections 1-2/3-5/6+ $20/31/38).

Boat

☑ **Best for...** Taronga Zoo, Balmain, Cockatoo Island, Watsons Bay and Manly.

➡ Most **Sydney Ferries** (☎131 500; www.transportnsw.info) boats operate between 6am and midnight. The standard single fare for most harbour destinations is $6.20; boats to Manly, Sydney Olympic Park and Parramatta cost $7.60.

➡ Private companies **Manly Fast Ferry** (☎02-9583 1199; www.manlyfastferry.com.au; adult/child $9/6) and **Sydney Fast Ferries** (☎02-9818 6000; www.sydneyfastferries.com.au; adult/child $9.75/7.50; 🕿) both offer boats that blast from Circular Quay to Manly in 18 minutes.

➡ Water taxis are a fast way to shunt around the harbour (Circular Quay to Watsons Bay in as little as 15 minutes). Companies will quote on any pick-up point within the harbour and the river, including private jetties, islands and other boats.

Light Rail

☑ **Best for...** Pyrmont & Glebe

➡ Trams run between Central and Dulwich Hill, stopping in Chinatown, Darling Harbour, the Star casino, Sydney Fish Market and Glebe en route.

➡ Tickets cost $3.80 for a short journey and $4.80 for a longer one, and can be purchased from the conductor.

Taxi

☑ **Best for...** Short trips around town.

➡ Metered taxis are easy to flag down in the central city and inner suburbs,

Tickets & Passes

➡ Although you can still buy individual tickets for most public transport services, a smartcard system called **Opal** (www.opal.com.au) also operates.

➡ The card can be obtained (for free) and loaded with credit at numerous newsagencies and convenience stores across Sydney.

➡ When commencing and completing a journey you'll need to touch the card to an electronic reader.

➡ Advantages include cheaper single journeys, daily charges capped at $15 ($2.50 on Sundays) and free travel after taking any eight journeys in a week (it resets itself every Monday). You can use the Opal card at the airport train stations, but none of the aforementioned bonuses apply.

➡ Paper-based **MyMulti** passes can be purchased at ferry and train ticket offices and many newsagencies and convenience stores, but you're much better off getting an Opal card. For instance, the MyMulti Day Pass costs $24 as opposed to the $15 Opal cap.

except for at changeover times (3pm and 3am).

→ Fares are regulated, so all companies charge the same. Flagfall is $3.50, with a $2.50 'night owl surcharge' after 10pm on a Friday and Saturday until 6am the following morning. The fare thereafter is $2.14 per kilometre, with an additional surcharge of 20% between 10pm and 6am nightly. There's also a $2.40 fee for bookings.

→ The UberX ride-sharing app operates in Sydney but the state government maintains that it is illegal for drivers to offer the service.

→ For more on Sydney's taxis, see www.nswtaxi.org.au.

Reliable Operators

Legion Cabs (☎13 14 51; www.legioncabs.com.au)

Premier Cabs (☎13 10 17; www.premiercabs.com.au)

RSL Cabs (☎02-9581 1111; www.rslcabs.com.au)

Taxis Combined (☎133 300; www.taxiscombined.com.au)

Car & Motorcycle

☑ **Best for...** Getting to the beaches quickly.

→ Avoid driving in central Sydney if you can: there's a confusing one-way street system, parking is expensive (even at hotels), and parking inspectors and tow-away zones proliferate.

→ Conversely, a car is handy for accessing Sydney's outer reaches (particularly the beaches) and for day trips.

→ For 24-hour emergency roadside assistance, maps, travel advice, insurance and accommodation discounts, contact the **National Roads & Motorists Association** (NRMA; ☎132 132; www.nrma.com.au; 74 King St; ⊙9am-5pm Mon-Fri; ☒Wynyard). It has reciprocal arrangements with similar organisations interstate and overseas (bring proof of membership).

Driving

→ Australians drive on the left-hand side of the road.

→ The minimum driving age is 18.

→ Overseas visitors can drive with their domestic

driving licences for up to three months but must obtain a NSW driving licence after that.

→ Speed limits in Sydney are generally 60km/h (50km/h in some areas), rising to 100km/h or 110km/h on motorways.

→ Seat belts are compulsory; using hand-held mobile phones is prohibited.

→ A blood-alcohol limit of 0.05% is enforced with random breath tests and hefty punishments. If you're in an accident (even if you didn't cause it) and you're over the alcohol limit, your insurance will be invalidated.

Parking

→ Sydney's private car parks are expensive (around $15 per hour); public car parks are more affordable (sometimes under $10 per hour).

→ The city centre and Darling Harbour have the greatest number of private car parks, but these are also the priciest.

→ Street parking meters devour coins (from $2.50 to $5 per hour) and some take credit cards.

Toll Roads

➧ Sydney's motorways are all tolled; charges vary with the distance travelled – anywhere from $2 to $15.

➧ Most toll roads are cash-less; hire-car companies can provide information on setting up a temporary electronic pass.

Hire

➧ Car rental prices vary depending on season and demand.

➧ Read the small print to check age restrictions, exactly what your insurance covers and where you can take the car (dirt roads are sometimes off limits).

➧ The big players have airport desks and city offices (mostly around William St).

➧ For motorbike hire, try **Bikescape** (☎02-9569 4111; www.bikescape.com.au; cnr Parramatta Rd & Young St, Annandale; tours from $195; ☒Stanmore).

Bicycle

☑ **Best for...** Keeping fit and seeing stuff.

➧ Sydney traffic can be intimidating, but there are an increasing number

of dedicated separate bike lanes; see www.cityofsydney.nsw.gov.au.

➧ Helmets are compulsory.

➧ There's no charge for taking a bike on CityRail trains, except during peak hours (6am to 9am and 3.30pm to 7.30pm Monday to Friday) when you will need to purchase a child's ticket for the bike.

➧ Bikes travel for free on Sydney's ferries, which usually have bicycle racks (first come, first served).

➧ Buses are no-go zones for bikes.

Essential Information

Business Hours

Restaurants noon-3pm & 6-10pm

Cafes 8am-4pm

Pubs 11am-midnight Monday to Saturday, 11am-10pm Sunday

Shops 9.30am-6pm Monday to Wednesday, Friday & Saturday, 9.30am-8pm Thursday, 11am-5pm Sunday

Banks 9.30am-4pm Monday to Thursday, 9.30am-5pm Friday

Discount Cards

➧ **Sydney Museums Pass** (www.sydneylivingmuseums.com.au/sydney-museums-pass; adult/child $18/9) Allows a single visit to four boutique museums: Museum of Sydney, Hyde Park Barracks, Justice & Police Museum and Susannah Place. It's valid for three months and available at each of the participating museums.

➧ **Ultimate Sydney Pass** (adult/child $99/70) Provides access to the attractions operated by Merlin Entertainment: Sydney Tower Eye (including the Skywalk), Sydney Sea Life Aquarium, Wild Life Sydney Zoo, Madame Tussauds and Manly Sea Life Sanctuary. It's available from each of the venues, but is often considerably cheaper online. If you plan on visiting only some of these attractions, discounted **Sydney Attractions Passes** are available in any combination you desire.

Electricity

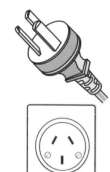

240V/50Hz

Emergency

Call ☎000 for police, ambulance or fire brigade.

Money

☑ **Top Tip** Travellers cheques are something of a dinosaur these days, and they won't be accepted everywhere. It's easier not to bother with them.

➡ The unit of currency is the Australian dollar, which is divided into 100 cents.

➡ Notes are colourful, plastic and washing-machine-proof, in denominations of $100, $50, $20, $10 and $5.

➡ Coins come in $2, $1, 50¢, 20¢, 10¢ and 5¢. The old 2¢ and 1¢ coins have been out of circulation for years, so shops round prices up (or down) to the nearest 5¢. Curiously, $2 coins are smaller than $1.

ATMs

➡ Central Sydney is chock-full of banks with 24-hour ATMs that will accept debit and credit cards linked to international network systems (Cirrus, Maestro, Visa, MasterCard etc).

➡ Most banks place a $1000 limit on the amount you can withdraw daily.

➡ You'll also find ATMs in pubs and clubs, although these usually charge slightly higher fees.

➡ Shops and retail outlets usually have Eftpos facilities, which allow you to pay for purchases with your debit or credit card.

Credit Cards

➡ Visa and MasterCard are widely accepted at larger shops, restaurants and hotels, but not necessarily at smaller shops or cafes.

➡ Diners Club and American Express are less widely accepted.

Money Changers

➡ Exchange bureaux are dotted around the city centre, Kings Cross and Bondi.

➡ Shop around as rates vary and most outlets charge some sort of commission.

➡ The counters at the airport are open until the last flight comes in; rates here aren't quite as good as they are in the city.

Tipping

In Sydney, most services don't expect a tip, so you shouldn't feel pressured into giving one. If the service is good, however, it is customary to tip wait staff in restaurants (up to 10%) and taxi drivers (round up to the nearest dollar).

Public Holidays

☑ **Top Tip** Most public holidays cleverly morph into long weekends (three days), so if a holiday such as New Year's Day falls on a weekend, the following Monday is usually a holiday.

On public holidays, government departments, banks, offices and post

Money-Saving Tips

➡ While there's no such thing as a free lunch at Sydney's fine-dining restaurants, you can save a pretty penny at some of them if you know when to go. Keep an eye out for set-price lunch specials and pre-theatre menus.

➡ For views, put on your glad rags and zip up to Blu Bar on the 36th floor of the Shangri-La hotel (p39) or O Bar (p62) on the rotating 47th floor of the Australia Square tower. They're not cheap bars, but a cocktail will cost less than the price of visiting Sydney Tower.

➡ Rather than booking an expensive harbour cruise, grab a ferry to Manly to explore the outer harbour and a Parramatta river service to head upstream.

offices shut up shop. On Good Friday, Easter Sunday, Anzac Day and Christmas Day, most shops are closed. Public holidays include the following:

New Year's Day 1 January

Australia Day 26 January

Easter (Good Friday to Easter Monday) March/April

Anzac Day 25 April

Queen's Birthday Second Monday in June

Bank Holiday First Monday in August (only banks are closed)

Labour Day First Monday in October

Christmas Day 25 December

Boxing Day 26 December

Something else to consider when planning

a Sydney visit is school holidays, when accommodation rates soar and everything gets decidedly hectic. Sydney students have a long summer break that includes Christmas and most of January. Other school holidays fall around March to April (Easter), late June to mid-July, and late September to early October.

Telephone

☑ **Top Tip** Toll-free numbers start with the prefix ✆1800, while numbers that start with ✆1300 are charged at the cost of a local call.

➡ Public telephones, which can be found all over the city, take phonecards, credit cards and occasionally (if the coin slots aren't jammed up) coins.

➡ Australia's country code: ✆61

➡ Sydney's area code: ✆02 (drop the zero when dialling into Australia)

➡ International access code: ✆0011 (used when dialling other countries from Australia)

Mobile Phones

➡ Australian mobile phone numbers have four-digit prefixes starting with ✆04.

➡ Australia's digital network is compatible with most international phones, with the exception being some phones from the USA and Japan. Quad-band US/Japanese phones will work, but if you want to use an Australian SIM card, you'll need an unlocked handset.

Tourist Information

☑ **Top Tip** Opening hours for information centres vary with the seasons; summer hours may be longer than those listed here.

Sydney Visitor Centres

Sydney's main visitors centres come with walls of brochures and information on Sydney and regional NSW. Knowledgeable staff can help you find a hotel or a restaurant with harbour views, book a tour, hire a car and arrange transport for day trips out of town. Branches in the **Rocks** (☎02-8273 0000; www. bestof.com.au; cnr Argyle & Playfair Sts; ☒Circular Quay) and **Darling Harbour** (☎02-8273 0000; www. bestof.com.au; Palm Grove, behind IMAX; ⊕9.30am-5.30pm; ☒Town Hall).

City Host Information

Kiosks Branches in **Circular Quay** (Map p30; www.cityofsydney.nsw.gov.au; cnr Pitt & Alfred Sts; ⊕9am-5pm; ☒Circular Quay), **Haymarket** (Map p52; www.cityofsydney.nsw.gov. au; Dixon St; ⊕11am-7pm; ☒Town Hall), **Kings Cross** (www.cityofsydney.nsw.gov. au; cnr Darlinghurst Rd &

Springfield Ave; ⊕9am-5pm; ☒Kings Cross) and **Town Hall** (www.cityofsydney.nsw. gov.au; George St; ⊕9am-5pm; ☒Town Hall). **Hello Manly** (Map p150; ☎02-9976 1430; www.hello manly.com.au; Manly Wharf; ⊕9am-5pm; 🚢Manly) This helpful visitors centre, just outside the ferry wharf and alongside the bus interchange, has free pamphlets covering the Manly Scenic Walkway and other Manly attractions, plus loads of local bus information.

Travellers with Disabilities

☑ **Top Tip** Some taxis accommodate wheelchairs – request them when you make your booking.

➡ Compared with many other major cities, Sydney has great access for citizens and visitors with disabilities.

➡ Most of Sydney's main attractions are accessible by wheelchair, and all new or renovated buildings must, by law, include wheelchair access. Older buildings can pose some problems, however, and some restaurants and entertainment venues

aren't quite up to scratch. Most of the National Trust's historic houses are at least partially accessible.

➡ Most of Sydney's major attractions offer hearing loops and sign-language interpreters for hearing-impaired travellers. To expedite proceedings, contact venue staff in advance.

➡ Many new buildings incorporate architectural features that are helpful to the vision impaired, such as textured floor details at the top and bottom of stairs. Sydney's pedestrian crossings feature catchy beep-and-buzz sound cues.

Organisations

City of Sydney (☎02-9265 9333; www.cityofsydney. nsw.gov.au) Lists parking spaces, transport information, CBD access maps and other information.

Deaf Society of NSW (☎TTY 02-8833 3691; www. deafsocietynsw.org.au)

Roads & Maritime (☎13 22 13; www.rms.nsw.gov. au) Supplies temporary parking permits for international drivers with disabilities.

Spinal Cord Injuries Australia (SCIA; ☎1800 819 775; www.spinalcord injuries.com.au)

Vision Australia (☎1300 847 466; www.visionaustralia. org)

Visas

☑ **Top Tip** All visitors to Australia need a visa – only New Zealand nationals are exempt, and even they receive a 'special category' visa on arrival.

➡ Visa application forms are available from Australian diplomatic missions overseas, travel agents or the website of the **Department of Immigration & Citizenship** (DIAC; ☎13 18 81; www.immi. gov.au).

➡ Citizens of EU member countries, Andorra, Iceland, Liechtenstein, Monaco, Norway, San Marino and Switzerland are eligible for an **eVisitor**, which is free and allows visitors to stay in Australia for up to three months. eVisitors must be applied for online and are electronically stored and linked to individual passport numbers, so no stamp in your passport is required. Apply at least 14 days prior to the proposed date of travel to Australia. Applications are made on the Department of Immigration & Citizenship website.

➡ An **Electronic Travel Authority (ETA)** allows visitors to enter Australia anytime within a 12-month period and stay for up to three months at a time (unlike eVisitor, multiple entries are permitted). Travellers from qualifying countries can get an ETA through any International Air Transport Association (IATA)–registered travel agent or overseas airline. They make the application for you when you buy a ticket and issue the ETA, which replaces the usual visa stamped in your passport. It's common practice for travel agents to charge a fee for issuing an ETA (in the vicinity of US$25). This system is available to passport holders of some 33 countries, including all of the countries that are eligible for eVisitor.

➡ The eight countries that are eligible for ETA but not eVisitor can make their application online at www.eta.immi. gov.au, where a $20 fee applies. Those countries are Brunei, Canada, Hong Kong, Japan, Malaysia, Singapore, South Korea and the USA.

➡ If you are from a country not covered by eVisitor or ETA, or you want to stay longer than three months, you'll need to apply for a visa. **Tourist visas** cost from $130 and allow single or multiple entry for stays of three, six or 12 months and are valid for use within 12 months of issue.

Index

See also separate subindexes for:

Eating p195

Drinking p196

Entertainment p196

Shopping p197

Sights 000
Map Pages **000**

Sights 000

Map Pages **000**

Behind the Scenes

Send Us Your Feedback

We love to hear from travellers – your comments help make our books better. We read every word, and we guarantee that your feedback goes straight to the authors. Visit **lonelyplanet.com/contact** to submit your updates and suggestions.

Note: We may edit, reproduce and incorporate your comments in Lonely Planet products such as guidebooks, websites and digital products, so let us know if you don't want your comments reproduced or your name acknowledged. For a copy of our privacy policy visit lonelyplanet.com/privacy.

Peter's Thanks

I owe a great debt of thanks to all my Sydney support crew, particularly David Mills, Barry Sawtell, Tony Dragicevich, Debbie Debono, Tim Moyes and Michael Woodhouse. Thanks for sacrificing your stomachs and livers so enthusiastically for this book.

Acknowledgments

Cover photograph: Sydney Opera House; Shaun Egan/AWL

Photograph on pp4-5: Sydney Opera House and the Harbour Bridge; Andrew Watson/Getty

This Book

This 4th edition of Lonely Planet's *Pocket Sydney* was researched and written by Peter Dragicevich, who also wrote the previous edition. This guidebook was produced by the following:

Destination Editor Tasmin Waby **Product Editors** Jenna Myers, Katie O'Connell **Regional Senior Cartographer** Mark Griffiths **Book Designer** Virginia Moreno **Assisting Editors** Imogen Bannister, Anne Mulvaney, Simon Williamson **Cover**

Researcher Naomi Parker **Thanks to** Sasha Baskett, Daniel Corbett, Anna Harris, Kate Kiely, Claire Naylor, Karyn Noble, Sarah Reid, Ellie Simpson, Angela Tinson, Lauren Wellicome, Amanda Williamson

Our Writer

Peter Dragicevich

After a decade of frequent flights between his native New Zealand and Sydney, the lure of the bright lights and endless beach days drew Peter across the Tasman on a more permanent basis. For the best part of the next decade he would call Sydney's inner suburbs home, while managing the city's most popular gay and lesbian newspaper, followed by a stable of upmarket food, fashion and photography magazines. More recently he's co-authored dozens of titles for Lonely Planet, including two previous editions of this guide and five other Australian titles.

Published by Lonely Planet Publications Pty Ltd
ABN 36 005 607 983
4th edition – Dec 2015
ISBN 978 1 74321 013 0
© Lonely Planet 2015   Photographs © as indicated 2015
10 9 8 7 6 5 4 3 2 1
Printed in China